Transitional Kindergarten
IMPLEMENTATION GUIDE

A Resource for California Public School District Administrators and Teachers

Governor's State Advisory Council on Early Learning and Care

Sacramento • 2013

Publishing Information

The *Transitional Kindergarten Implementation Guide: A Resource for California Public School District Administrators and Teachers* was developed by the Child Development Division of the California Department of Education (CDE), under contract with the Sacramento County Office of Education. The document was edited by John McLean and Faye Ong, working in cooperation with Erin Dubey, Consultant, Child Development Division. It was published by the California Department of Education, 1430 N Street, Sacramento, CA 95814-5901, and was distributed under the provisions of the Library Distribution Act and Government Code Section 11096.

ISBN: 978-0-8011-1744-2

CDE Publications and Educational Resources

For information about publications and educational resources available from the California Department of Education (CDE), visit http://www.cde.ca.gov/re/pn/rc/ or call the CDE Press sales office at 1-800-995-4099.

Notice

The guidance in the *Transitional Kindergarten Implementation Guide: A Resource for California Public School District Administrators and Teachers* is not binding on local educational agencies or other entities. Except for statutes, regulations, and court decisions referenced herein, the document is exemplary, and compliance with it is not mandatory. (See *Education Code* Section 33308.5.)

Contents

A Message from the State Advisory Council on Early Learning and Care

We are pleased to present the *Transitional Kindergarten Implementation Guide: A Resource for California Public School District Administrators and Teachers*, a publication we believe will be valuable to local educational agencies as they implement transitional kindergarten (TK) programs. Building upon the *Transitional Kindergarten (TK) Planning Guide* published in 2011 by the California County Superintendents Educational Services Association, this publication provides resources and guidance in the areas of program design, curriculum, instruction, assessment, and family/community partnerships.

The TK implementation guide focuses on the essential components for school district administrators and teachers to consider as they develop comprehensive TK programs. The first chapter of the guide focuses on considerations for the structure and design of TK programs. Chapters 2–8 provide a more in-depth discussion of effective instructional and curricular approaches, including the importance of family and community partnerships and systems of support for transitional kindergarten.

We express our gratitude to teachers, administrators, and early care and education experts who provided extensive feedback on the development of the *Transitional Kindergarten Implementation Guide*. We also extend our appreciation to the teachers who served on the TK/K Advisory Committee to share their expertise in the development of the guide and the video illustrations that accompany it. In addition, we thank the local educational agency representatives and parents who shared their experiences through interviews and provided access for videotaping TK classrooms and activities. We are especially grateful to the Sacramento County Office of Education and its subcontractors for coordinating and leading the effort to provide California's public school district administrators and teachers with these valuable TK resources.

PETE CERVINKA
California Department of Social Services
*Co-Chair, State Advisory Council on
Early Learning and Care*

LUPITA CORTEZ ALCALÁ
California Department of Education
*Co-Chair, State Advisory Council on
Early Learning and Care*

List of Members:
State Advisory Council on
Early Learning and Care

Co-Chairs

Pete Cervinka, Program Deputy Director of Benefits and Services
   California Department of Social Services

Lupita Cortez Alcalá, Deputy Superintendent of Public Instruction
   California Department of Education

Camille Maben, Executive Director
   First 5 California (former Co-Chair)

Members

Nancy Bargmann, Deputy Director, Community Operations Division
   California Department of Developmental Services

Magdalena Carrasco, Commissioner
   First 5 California

Julian Crocker, Superintendent of Schools
   San Luis Obispo County

Sydney Fisher Larson, Professor, Early Childhood Education
   College of the Redwoods

Mark Friedman, Executive Director
   First 5 Alameda County

Linda James Perry, Head Start Director
   Long Beach Unified School District

Katie Johnson, Assistant Secretary
   California Health and Human Services Agency

Nancy Remley, Director
   Head Start State Collaboration Office

Ryan Storm, Assistant Program Budget Manager
   California Department of Finance

Natalie Woods Andrews, Director, School Readiness Department
   Sacramento County Office of Education

Acknowledgments

The *Transitional Kindergarten Implementation Guide* was developed with contributions from many people and organizations. We gratefully acknowledge the efforts of the individuals and entities named below.

Project Leaders

Natalie Woods Andrews, EdD, Director,
   School Readiness Department,
   Sacramento County Office of Education

Nancy Herota, Director,
   School Readiness Department,
   Sacramento County Office of Education

Writers (Staff Members and Consultants from the Sacramento County Office of Education)

Jennifer Gonzalez, Key Writer

Kelly Twibell Sanchez, Key Writer

Elizabeth Pinkerton, Editing Assistance

Natalie Woods Andrews, EdD

Karen Hayashi

Nancy Herota

Jan Mayer, EdD

Kathleen Sadao, EdD

Transitional Kindergarten / Kindergarten Teacher Advisory Committee

Barbara Blakely, Retired Transitional
   Kindergarten/Kindergarten Teacher

Elizabeth Magruder, Transitional
   Kindergarten Consultant

Lisa Peterson, Transitional Kindergarten
   Teacher, Clovis Unified School District

Vera Refnes, Retired Kindergarten Teacher

Vara Tanner-Palmero, Transitional Kindergarten
   Teacher, Rescue Union School District

Heather Wright, Kindergarten Teacher,
   Elk Grove Unified School District

Local Educational Agencies

The following local educational agencies are recognized for their contributions, which included allowing interviews of transitional kindergarten staff members and video illustrations of transitional kindergarten classrooms:

Clovis Unified School District

Fresno Unified School District

Gilroy Unified School District

Junction Elementary School District

Kingsburg Elementary Charter School District

Livingston Union School District

Long Beach Unified School District

Mariposa County Unified School District

Merced City School District

Merced County Office of Education

Pasadena Unified School District

Placentia–Yorba Linda Unified School District

Rescue Union School District

Sacramento City Unified School District

California Department of Education

Cecelia Fisher-Dahms, Administrator,
   Quality Improvement Office,
   Child Development Division

Erin Dubey, Consultant,
   Child Development Division

Carrie Roberts, Administrator,
   Professional Learning Support Division

Kathleen Halvorson, Consultant,
   Professional Learning Support Division

Erin Koepke, Consultant,
   Professional Learning Support Division

Meredith Cathcart, Administrator,
   Special Education Division

Special thanks are extended to the crew of **Iron Mountain Films, Inc.**, for video production.

Note: The names, titles, and affiliations of the individuals listed in these acknowledgments were current at the time the publication was developed.

INTRODUCTION

Introduction Interviews and Classroom Video
http://www4.scoe.net/ims/webcasts/cf/index.
cfm?fuseaction=archivedDetail&eventID=140&archiveID=249

Introduction Interviews and Classroom Video (YouTube with Captions)
http://www.youtube.com/watch?v=wiqY8cbqfj0

The California Kindergarten Readiness Act of 2010, authored as Senate Bill (SB) 1381 by State Senator Joseph Simitian, will have a significant impact on children who have the opportunity to enroll in transitional kindergarten (TK) programs. SB 1381 implemented a gradual, phased-in conversion of the month and day by which a child must turn five years of age in order to be eligible for kindergarten, changing that date from December 2 to September 1 over a three-year period. Beginning in 2012–13, school districts were required to offer a TK program for children whose fifth birthday fell between November 2 and December 2. The kindergarten age entry requirement moves back one month over a three-year period, so that by 2014–15 and each year thereafter, children must be five years of age on or before September 1 to be eligible for kindergarten. The law also required school districts to develop a transitional kindergarten program for children who will no longer be age-eligible for kindergarten. Transitional kindergarten is the first year of a two-year program that provides a "modified kindergarten curriculum that is age and developmentally appropriate" (*Education Code* Section 48000).

History of Kindergarten

Early childhood education policies in California had their roots in the kindergarten movement of the nineteenth century. The first private kindergarten in California was developed in San Francisco on September 10, 1863, during a time when very few kindergarten programs existed in the United States. By 1888, 40 kindergarten programs were operating in San Francisco with approximately 4,500 children attending the classes—a reality that gained the attention of policymakers and other community advocates (de Cos 2001).

Along with the expansion of kindergarten programs during this era, the evolution of kindergarten teacher training programs was another important development in the history of the kindergarten reform movement. A key step to professionalize the field was the establishment in 1896 of a department for training kindergarten teachers at the State Normal School in Los Angeles, which eventually became the University of California, Los Angeles. In 1900–01, state legislation was passed to provide kindergarten primary certification for graduates of the State Normal School in Los Angeles and other kindergarten training institutions approved by the State Board of Education. Following this legislation, the Normal School of California established a teacher training program in 1920 that combined kindergarten and the primary grades, thus allowing teachers to work in any of these grade levels and advancing the movement for kindergarten to become integrated into the public schools (de Cos 2001).

Beyond the development of teacher training programs, other critical policy issues that supported the expansion of public kindergarten were legislation and funding. In 1913, at a time when only 14 counties in California had kindergarten in place, the California Legislature passed a law to allow local school boards to create kindergarten for children between the ages of four years and six and a half years (Ross 1976). The law was amended in 1915 to allow school districts to impose a local tax to support the expansion of kindergarten. By 1918, California was leading the other states, ranking ninth in the nation in the number of children between the ages of four and six who were enrolled in public kindergarten.

In November 1946, California voters approved a constitutional amendment to make kindergarten a part of the elementary school system through state funding. Although kindergarten remained voluntary for parents, the Legislature made a change in 1967 to require school districts to incorporate kindergarten programs for children who were eligible for enrollment. Currently, while enrollment in kindergarten remains voluntary, between 91 percent and 95 percent of age-eligible children in California attend private or public kindergarten (de Cos 2001). Additionally, although school districts are required to offer transitional kindergarten programs, attendance in these programs is also voluntary. However, in accordance with *Education Code* Section 48200, children must be enrolled in school by age six.

Prior to the passage of SB 1381, there were several legislative attempts to move back the date for kindergarten entry, as California was one of only four states with kindergarten-entry birthdates in December. Though previous attempts to pass legislation failed, Assembly Bill (AB) 25 was enacted into law in 2000 to allow school districts to pilot the effectiveness of changing the cutoff date for kindergarten to September 1. AB 25 had little impact on this policy issue, as the legislation did not provide funding for school districts to test the approach. A report from Governor Schwarzenegger's Committee on Education Excellence (2007) also made a recommendation to change the kindergarten cutoff date to September 1. However, no immediate actions resulted from this recommendation until the passage of SB 1381.

Rationale for Transitional Kindergarten

Research indicates that SB 1381 will have a positive effect on preparing California's children for kindergarten readiness and success beyond the primary grades. Entering kindergarten at an older age is one early predictor for student success. As Cannon and Lipscomb have stated, "Students who are older when they enter kindergarten have better elementary math and reading scores . . . These effects appear to persist into eighth grade, albeit with smaller magnitudes" (Cannon and Lipscomb 2008, 1).

Starting kindergarten at an older age will also allow children to further develop their social and emotional skills and be ready to actively engage in academics at the kindergarten level. Because of the increasing academic demands placed on kindergarten students, there is less and less time

to nurture social and emotional skills. Deficiencies in these areas tend to inhibit learning in younger kindergarten students, which causes them to fall behind academically. Joseph Durlak and his colleagues (2011) state, "Emotions can facilitate or impede children's academic engagement, work ethic, commitment, and ultimate school success" (Durlak et al. 2011, 405). As a result, by the time these same students enter first grade, they are more likely to be considered for retention, receive interventions, or be referred for special education testing.

Overview of the Transitional Kindergarten Implementation Guide

This guide is organized into two sections. The first section focuses on recommendations for the design and structure of TK programs that school districts might consider when planning for full implementation. This information is covered in chapter 1. The second section, chapters 2 through 8, covers the following topics: (a) The Transitional Kindergarten Student, (b) Curriculum in a Transitional Kindergarten Program, (c) Effective Instruction in a Transitional Kindergarten Program, (d) The Transitional Kindergarten Learning Environment, (e) Assessment and Differentiated Instruction in the Transitional Kindergarten Classroom, (f) Involving Families and Community Partners in a Transitional Kindergarten Program, and (g) Supporting Transitional Kindergarten Implementation. Although each program component is addressed in a separate chapter, they are all interrelated and each impacts the others in critical ways. TK teachers, administrators, and support staff understand the critical attributes of individual components, and they recognize and consistently reinforce the powerful interaction of the components as they intentionally plan and deliver instruction. For example:

- The TK learning environment is reflective of the TK curriculum, students' developmental levels, and their educational strengths, interests, and assessed needs.

- Decisions about instructional strategies are based on evidence from assessments and are responsive to the developmental and educational levels of students.

- Parent support and engagement strongly impacts student performance, influences the structure of the learning environment, and can influence instructional planning (e.g., opportunities for small-group instruction).

- Effective professional development has the potential for impacting all program components.

- Assessment informs both curriculum and instructional decisions. It strongly impacts students and their progress as opportunities for differentiation are based on assessed needs.

CHAPTER 1
Program Structure and Design

Program Structure and Design
http://www4.scoe.net/ims/webcasts/cf/index.
cfm?fuseaction=archivedDetail&eventID=140&archiveID=250

Program Structure and Design (YouTube with Captions)
http://www.youtube.com/watch?v=_w40nuCH7IE

California Senate Bill 1381, the Kindergarten Readiness Act of 2010, allows for school districts to design a transitional kindergarten (TK) program to meet local needs. The goal of a high-quality TK program is to provide extended opportunities for socialization and learning. It is recommended that school districts address all areas of program structure and design, including (a) Policy Development, (b) Funding, (c) Staffing Qualifications, (d) Class Configuration/Schedules, (e) Universal Design for Learning, (f) Special Education Services, and (g) English Learners.

Policy Development

School districts have flexibility to design TK programs that meet local needs, and as a result, they may develop policies for the implementation of TK in a variety of areas. Policy considerations might include age criteria for placement, early admissions, acceleration into first grade, and transportation. One key policy decision for school districts to address is the age criteria for enrolling students in TK classes. Based on the gradual age requirement changes that are taking place over a three-year period, school districts may adopt plans to phase in the enrollment of TK students. In 2012–13, many districts followed the age criteria established by law and enrolled TK students whose fifth birthday fell between November 2 and December 2. In other districts, policies were developed to enroll the cohort of all TK age-eligible students whose fifth birthday fell between September 2 and December 2.

Funding

Transitional kindergarten is considered the first year of a two-year kindergarten program. Therefore, school districts receive average daily attendance (ADA) funding for students enrolled in TK classes as they do for students enrolled in traditional kindergarten. In addition to ADA funding, the following funding streams can support TK classrooms.

Title 1, Elementary and Secondary Education Act—Education for the Disadvantaged

Title I, Part A, of the No Child Left Behind (NCLB) Act of 2001 is intended to help ensure that all children have the opportunity to obtain a high-quality education and to reach proficiency on challenging state academic standards and assessments. Title I, Part A, provides supplemental funding that may be used to provide additional instructional staff, professional development, parental involvement, extended-time programs, and other support for raising student achievement in high-poverty schools (California Department of Education [CDE] 2013d).

Title II, Elementary and Secondary Education Act—Preparing, Training, and Recruiting High-Quality Teachers and Principals

The purpose of Title II, Part A, is to increase the academic achievement of all students by helping schools and districts improve teacher and principal quality and ensure that all teachers are highly qualified. Title II, Part A, provides local educational agencies (LEAs) with the flexibility to use these funds creatively to address challenges to teacher quality, whether they concern teacher preparation and qualifications of new teachers, recruitment and hiring, induction, professional development, teacher retention, or the need for more capable principals and assistant principals to serve as effective school leaders (U.S. Department of Education 2006).

Title III, Elementary and Secondary Education Act—Language Instruction for Limited English Proficient and Immigrant Students (CDE 2012d)

Immigrant Education Program funds are to be specifically targeted to eligible immigrant students and their families through the provision of supplementary programs and services for the underlying purpose of assuring that these students meet the same challenging grade-level and graduation standards as mainstream students.

The purpose of *Title III* Immigrant Education Program subgrants is to pay for enhanced instructional opportunities to immigrant students and their families. LEAs may choose from activities authorized by *Title III*:

- Family literacy, parent training, and community outreach

- Funding of educational personnel, including teacher aides

- Tutorials, mentoring, and counseling

- Identification and acquisition of educational materials and technology

- Basic instructional services

- Other instructional services designed to assist immigrant students to achieve in elementary and secondary schools in the United States

- Activities coordinated with community-based organizations (CBOs), institutions of higher education (IHEs), or private sector entities that have expertise in working with immigrant students and their families

Staffing Qualifications

TK classrooms, as mandated in statute, are to be staffed by credentialed teachers or holders of teaching permits that authorize general education instruction in self-contained classrooms for the grade levels of kindergarten (California Commission on Teacher Credentialing 2011). Additionally, programs with children identified as English learners must be staffed by teachers who are qualified to deliver English learner instructional

services. Qualifications include possession of the Crosscultural, Language, and Academic Development (CLAD) certificate, which authorizes a person to teach English language development (ELD) and specially designed academic instruction in English (SDAIE). Bilingual Authorization authorizes teachers to provide primary language instruction in addition to ELD and SDAIE. Teachers may obtain the authorizations to teach English learners through course work taken in a Commission on Teacher Credentialing–approved program or by passing the California Teachers of English Learners (CTEL) exam for a CLAD certificate and sections of the California Subject Examinations for Teachers (CSET) and the Languages Other Than English (LOTE) exams for a bilingual authorization. TK offers a unique and important opportunity to provide extended experiences for English language acquisition in the first year of a two-year kindergarten program. Specific strategies to support English learners are discussed in chapter 4.

Class Configuration/Schedules

TK classes must offer the same level of service offered for students enrolled in a traditional kindergarten program. The required minimum number of hours and days that pertain to kindergarten also apply to TK. TK self-contained classes can be offered through regional clusters or classes can be offered at multiple sites throughout the district. These decisions will be based on geographic needs, number of TK eligible students, facility availability and other related issues. Districts that choose to offer TK/K combination classes should consider the composition of the students in the class. Planning for a combination class may include a fairly balanced representation of TK and K students. On the other hand, planning for a TK/K combination class that includes two or three TK students where the majority are traditional kindergarten students, will require a different approach to ensure that TK students are exposed to a modified kindergarten curriculum that is age and developmentally appropriate (*Education Code* Section 48000). As in all highly effective classes, whether the combination class is fairly balanced or heavily weighted in one direction or the other, final decisions about classroom structure and instruction should be based on the assessed academic and social–emotional needs of each child. Effective approaches to implement a TK/K combination class are discussed in chapter 4.

Universal Design for Learning

A universal design for learning (UDL) approach can help TK teachers address the needs of diverse learners. UDL is a model borrowed from the field of architecture and has been implemented in the K–12 arena for the past 20 years (Center for Applied Special Technology 1999). One example of UDL is the availability of audio cues at street crossings, which allow people with visual impairments to safely navigate intersections. Not only do people with visual impairments benefit from the countdown of numbers to cross the street, but cyclists and other pedestrians are also helped by the estimation of time left for crossing. Most recently there have been applications to preschool and early childhood programs. The premise behind UDL revolves around creating accessible environments that work for all children. "This framework calls for early educators to value from the beginning the importance of planning learning environments and activities for a diverse population—creating universally designed settings in which all children and their families can participate and learn" (Conn-Powers et al. 2006, 2). The model is proactive in nature and requires TK teachers to consider curriculum and teaching strategies that promote learning through multiple lenses. Another example of UDL is selecting a curriculum and supplemental materials that provide options for reinforcement of initial lessons, a variety of seat work, direct and indirect instruction, additional assignments on the same topic, and hands-on activities with group support. The UDL model considers three principles for learning opportunities: (1) multiple means of engagement, (2) multiple means of representation, and (3) multiple means of expression. TK teachers should consider the individual interest levels and learning modalities of each student to ensure involvement in each lesson.

When a child is engaged in the learning activity, the TK teacher can vary the methods of instruction and the ways in which information is presented. Some students may work individually at their desks on a personal whiteboard, while others may be required to respond on the classroom whiteboard. Second, group assignments may present the information in activities and experiments that reinforce a science concept. Third, students may be offered a variety of ways to express what they have learned—for example, by raising their hand during a large-group session to comment on a book read or by recording their answer on a computer. Allowing for a variety of ways that children can demonstrate competency helps to differentiate the measurement of performance across student profiles. Incorporating inclusive practices that provide access and participatory means for students with disabilities is secondary to the initial UDL application. For example, all children benefit from clearly marked learning areas and picture-coded classroom schedules. Once UDL principles have been applied to the TK classroom, the need for more specific adaptations and supports is reduced. Inclusive practices are considered on a more individual level. For instance, in learning areas that are labeled with pictures and words, a child with a disability may have difficulty moving from one area to another. In this instance, the TK teacher may look to the individualized education program (IEP) and specialized instruction to add an individual visual schedule that will help the child transition between learning areas. UDL and inclusive practices work together to support the individual needs of students.

Special Education Services

It is important for parents, teachers, and administrators to discuss school placement options and address any questions or concerns. School support staff (e.g., specialists and school psychologists) can offer additional insight into the child's development as observed by parents and/ or teachers. The choice to enroll and participate in a TK program may be the most appropriate program placement for some kindergarten-eligible students. Research draws attention to other areas of concern such as children with disabilities being misdiagnosed as immature (Graue and DiPerna 2000) when perhaps they "should have been treated by some form of direct intervention other than delayed entry" (Katz 2000, 2). In making program decisions with families, school administrators and teachers are guided by the mandates of the Individuals with Disabilities Education Act (IDEA) concerning least restrictive environment (LRE) and nondiscrimination.

As a component of the public school system, the TK classroom abides by the various laws regarding public school attendance for young children who qualify by age for TK placement. In addition to serving students from diverse socioeconomic and ethnic/cultural backgrounds, the TK classroom teacher must consider and include students with disabilities who are age-eligible. Specific laws and regulations must be followed when a child with a disability is included in the TK classroom. The Individuals with Disabilities Education Act (IDEA) of 2004, Part B, mandates services for children with disabilities, ages three through twenty-one, who have been identified through assessment to warrant the need for special education (IDEA, 20 U.S.C., 1400 [2004]). The law specifies that special education and related services be provided as part of a free and appropriate public education, within the least restrictive environment determined by a multi-disciplinary team, including the parents, based on the child's individual learning needs.

Special education and related services are explored during the IEP meeting. During this meeting, special education and general education professionals and families review the assessment information and develop goals to be addressed. The IEP requires the team to document how the child will access the core curriculum and what supports will be needed. Additionally, the IEP helps TK teachers to understand the specific needs of the student and how to obtain the supports necessary for success. Special education and related services might include consultation from specialists, co-teaching opportunities with special educators, specially designed instruction, assistive technology devices and materials, specialized training events, team planning, and guidance. The IEP also indicates that student placement be based on the evaluation findings. As reiterated in a February 2012 letter to States from the director of the U.S. Department of Education's Office of Special Education Programs (Musgrove 2012), the IDEA includes the requirement that, to the maximum extent appropriate, students must be educated with peers of the same who have no disabilities. The law promotes the concept of inclusive practices in educating all children, including those with disabilities, within the general education classroom. Inclusion refers to the practice of ensuring that all children have access to the core curriculum and the development of social relationships within the classroom. As defined in the Division for Early Childhood (DEC) and National Association for the Education of Young Children (NAEYC) position statement on inclusion (DEC and NAEYC 2009), the key features of inclusion embody access to the learning setting and materials, participation in the learning activities, and supports for access and participation to occur. Once the child is assessed and placement in the least restrictive environment is determined by the IEP team, entrance into the TK classroom begins with UDL enhancements for all children, followed by individual considerations to ensure that the student's developmental needs are met.

English Learners

In 2012–13, more than 180,000 English learners began school in California's kindergarten classrooms, all of them bringing their own rich cultural and linguistic resources upon which to build their educational experiences (CDE 2013c). TK provides a tremendous opportunity for teachers to support young English learners by building on these experiences. TK also presents opportunities for these young students to learn new concepts and express themselves in their growing English repertoire.

TK teachers are instrumental in this process as they plan rich language experiences and provide extended opportunities to learn new vocabulary and to develop oral language skills. As they ease students' transition into a school setting and help make instruction more comprehensible for English learners, teachers can incorporate various techniques and strategies into classroom routines.

TK teachers have a new resource, the California English Language Development (ELD) Standards (CDE 2012b), to help them plan instruction for English learners. Adopted by the State Board of Education in November 2012, the ELD Standards provide background information and specific performance indicators for what English learners in kindergarten through grade 12 can do in English as they progress along a continuum of three proficiency levels (Emerging, Expanding, and Bridging). The ELD Standards can be used to plan for explicit language instruction for students at all ELD levels and to guide teachers in identifying and addressing language demands throughout the instructional day. Specific skills and examples of the language that students can produce at the three ELD levels are included, and can be readily incorporated into TK classrooms. The ELD Standards are aligned with the Common Core State Standards (CCSS) for English language arts, so instruction can be planned to use both sets of standards in tandem. Additionally, planning instruction coordinated with the ELD Standards will support students as teachers integrate other content areas.

Guidance from the ELD Standards and effective research-based practices highlight areas that are beneficial to English learners and can be incorporated into a TK program. These areas include (a) building connections through use of the student's primary language, (b) scaffolding instruction so that it is comprehensible for English learners, and (c) including explicit ELD instruction along with multiple opportunities for using English (Coleman and Goldenberg 2012; Hakuta and Santos 2012).

Building Connections

The strategic use of the student's primary language can be used to help them make connections to new content and build background knowledge and conceptual understanding. Explaining new ideas and school routines in a language that students readily understand will help provide a context for what they will learn in English, and it fosters their full participation in school experiences. Their primary language can be drawn upon in various ways. For example, teachers can pre-teach key vocabulary words and phrases before students listen to a story or expand students' understanding of new concepts through bilingual books. Additionally, teachers can provide parents and caregivers with ideas for how they may be able to expand on and reinforce the ideas being studied outside of school.

Comprehensible Instruction in English

TK teachers can enhance English learners' comprehension of information in English by regularly using visuals such as pictures, diagrams, charts, and realia so that students can understand new ideas while they are learning English (Espinosa 2010). At the beginning (emerging) stage of learning English, students can use physical responses to show that they understand what is being taught. For example, he or she can point to objects as requested or give one-word answers in response to questions by referring to a picture or chart. As students' language development progresses, they will be able to use longer phrases and expanded sentences with more details in English. Teachers can differentiate the level of support provided for each lesson, depending on the complexity of the academic task and the student's English proficiency level.

English Language Development

In addition to designing lessons that focus on English language development, TK teachers also play an important role in planning and supporting interactions with English-speaking peers who are valuable language models. Planning for activities in which English learners can interact with students who speak English will provide them with multiple opportunities for repetition of new language and additional practice in using English for a variety of purposes. To make the most of these opportunities, English learners should first be organized into small groups and explicitly taught the language they will need to perform the tasks. For example, key vocabulary can be introduced along with sentence stems that will help them to use new words (e.g., "I like to _____" or "May I use the _____?"). These strategies will foster students' confidence in using the language that they have had the opportunity to practice when interacting with peers in the classroom or on the playground. The day-to-day interactions and communication with peers during learning-area time and more structured small-group and whole-group experiences provide students with extended language development in natural settings.

English learners will have a successful TK experience when their linguistic and academic skills are supported and enhanced throughout the program. TK teachers have the opportunity to build the foundation for these students to experience success in school as they progress through the grade levels.

CHAPTER 2
The Transitional Kindergarten Student

The Transitional Kindergarten Student
http://www4.scoe.net/ims/webcasts/cf/index.
cfm?fuseaction=archivedDetail&eventID=140&archiveID=251

The Transitional Kindergarten Student (YouTube with Captions)
http://www.youtube.com/watch?v=Ry8uaS6H4fU

Although transitional kindergarten (TK) students are typically drawn from a chronologically homogeneous group, each student has a unique linguistic, cultural, and educational background. Awareness of individual development and learning needs is important as parents and teachers work together to determine the most appropriate education and support for young children. This chapter will provide an overview of the unique developmental, social–emotional and educational needs of TK students. Specific strategies for supporting social–emotional development and educational preparation are addressed in chapters 3 and 4.

Social–Emotional Development

Social–emotional development is foundational to academic learning (Hyson 2004; Raver 2002; Raver and Knitzer 2002; Zins et al. 2004) and is therefore an important area of focus in early education. To be successful in school, children must be confident in their ability to learn and build relationships with others (CSEFEL 2006). They need the ability to

Vignette

It is 15 minutes before the first day of school in Miss Minter's TK classroom. Miss Minter looks out the window and sees a few families waiting to enter the classroom. She notices a student with a look of concern on her face. "That's Ramich," she recalls to herself, as she observes the young girl holding tightly to her father's hand. "I remember her father shared with me at the school meet-and-greet that Ramich had never been to school before. I will make Ramich my helper today so that I can stay close to her and offer reassurance." Miss Minter turns to her daily schedule and reviews the activities she has planned. She knows that the pictures added to each activity will provide additional visual cues for following the daily routine. "Book reading with parents at tables, good-byes, welcome meeting, student choice . . ." Miss Minter is ready for her TK students. She has carefully read the California Preschool Learning Foundations, and she paid special attention to the Social–Emotional Development domain and the accompanying Preschool Curriculum Framework. TK will be a unique experience from her previous experiences with preschool and kindergarten classes. Miss Minter is ready to welcome all of her students, she knows what to expect of children at this age and stage of development, and most important, she is prepared to learn from her experiences with this richly diverse group of young students.

concentrate and persist in challenging tasks, develop listening skills, and attend to instructions.

Furthermore, children should be encouraged to be able to identify and communicate with others about emotions as well as solve social problems. In short, they must be socially and emotionally competent. Social–emotional competence includes four elements: emotional regulation, social knowledge and understanding, social skills, and social dispositions. *Emotional regulation* refers to children's ability to control behavior and respond appropriately to experiences. *Social knowledge* is the information about social norms and customs that enables children to participate successfully in the classroom community. *Social skills* are the appropriate strategies children apply when they interact with others. The environment and innate temperamental variations combine to create *social dispositions* (Epstein 2007).

TK students are dynamic learners. They are creative and inventive (Copple 2012). They develop persistence as they pursue self-initiated work, and they are growing in their ability to reason and solve problems. As students are developing the social and emotional competencies described above, students will exhibit different skills, strengths, needs, and areas for support. In addition, TK students who attended preschool programs will likely show familiarity with program routines and classroom rules. For other students, the TK environment will be their first introduction to formal classroom learning. TK teachers can

Social–Emotional Development and Educational Outcomes

A child's social–emotional competence influences current school achievement and is predictive of future academic learning (Thompson and Goodman 2009). Research demonstrates the importance of attending to and promoting student social and emotional development in early education:

- Children with poor social–emotional competence and self-regulation "have more difficulty transitioning to school" and are at greater risk for low academic achievement, behavioral problems, peer conflict and/or peer rejection, and school dropout (Committee for Children 2011, 2).

- Children's confidence and positive perception of themselves as learners, capable of growing in knowledge and skill, motivates them to pursue learning and persist through challenging tasks (Mueller and Dweck 1998; Galinsky 2010).

- Self-regulation abilities predict math and reading outcomes in the early elementary school years (National Institute of Child Health and Human Development [NICHD] Early Child Care Research Network 2003).

- Competence in understanding others' feelings has been associated with positive peer and adult relationships as well as academic achievement (Raver 2002; Raver and Knitzer 2002). Furthermore, individuals who are able to empathize and express care are "more actively engaged in the well-being of their classmates, teachers, and the greater school environment" (Thompson and Goodman 2009, 153).

- The quality of the teacher–student relationship serves as a regulatory function in social–emotional development and has a "potential to exert a positive or negative influence on children's ability to succeed in school" (Pianta and Stuhlman 2004, 445).

Educators who are knowledgeable about the importance of social–emotional development in early education intentionally plan curriculum and experiences to nurture student social–emotional competence.

anticipate that some students will experience separation anxiety as they say good-bye to family for the first time. A warm, nurturing approach can do much to offer reassurance and promote security in the TK classroom.

Positive Teacher–Student Relationships

Students who have positive relationships with their teachers do better in school and show resilience in confronting educational challenges (Pianta and Stuhlman 2004). They are eager to please and work diligently to meet expectations. This drive to succeed is a result of attentive commitment by the teacher to learn about each student's interests, learning styles, strengths, and the areas that need support. The TK teacher's effort to connect one-on-one has a powerful effect on the developing student. Even brief moments where the teacher pauses to observe, comment, and reflect with a student can do much to impact the child's development of a positive sense of self. As accomplished teachers know, taking the time to learn individual details about each student is an important start to building a meaningful connection.

How adults communicate with students is also important. Both verbal and nonverbal communications have significant impacts on relationships. Positive affect (e.g., a smile) and a simple gesture of friendliness (e.g., a "high five" or pat on the back) nurture a trusting relationship between a student and a teacher, and encourage students to push through difficult tasks. Offering detailed commentary (e.g., "I noticed you are adding a new level to your structure"), asking open-ended questions (e.g., "What ideas do you have for this section? Will you add windows to your structure?"), and then attentively listening to responses shows students that educators value their thoughts, ideas, and opinions.

Taking time to connect with students throughout the daily routine is a goal of all teachers; they make it a priority to ensure a significant encounter with each student at least once every week. A meaningful, shared moment can do much more to sustain and maintain important relationships than a passing, general comment. Teachers who spend quality time with students build meaningful connections that will shape future interactions and relationships for kindergarten and in later grades.

Positive Peer Relationships: Building a Classroom Community

As mentioned above, early education programs have an important impact on children's social skills and understanding (Epstein 2007). As children learn about themselves, they also make connections with others. They recognize how they are alike and different from others. They learn to take perspective, noting their peers' interests, opinions, and preferences. With support, children build new relationships and become active participants in the classroom community. As described in the *California Preschool Learning Foundations, Volume 3* (CDE 2013b), and the *California Preschool Curriculum Framework, Volume 3* (CDE 2013a), small- and large-group experiences provide ideal opportunities for students to develop a sense of community. Having a sense of community means seeing oneself as belonging to the group. Through their interactions with school staff and other students, young children deepen their understanding of social norms and conventions. These early life lessons prepare children to become "informed and engaged citizens of their country and of the world" (Koralek and Mindes 2006, 3).

TK teachers can do much to set the tone for community. Using phrases like "our class," "our group," "all of us," or "all together" communicates to students that they belong and creates an atmosphere in which students are expected to be kind and supportive of one another (Thompson and Twibell 2009). Educators may draw attention to occasions when students initiate or complete community work together (e.g., "We put everything away at cleanup time so that we have a place to learn together"). Class meetings offer regular opportunities to promote group discovery and decision making. TK teachers may gather students to introduce new small-group activities (e.g., "There is a new math game in our Math and Manipulatives Area. You need four friends to play the game"); plan upcoming events (e.g., "What do you want to learn more about when we study caterpillars?"); share important collaborative work (e.g., "Let's listen to Shayna and Taiga as they tell us about their science

experiment"); and resolve classroom challenges (e.g., "There have been a lot of friends pushing each other on the way out to recess. How can we keep each other safe when we walk together outside?").

Social–Emotional Curricula

TK administrators and teachers might also consider adopting a social–emotional curriculum to assist in the preparation and delivery of engaging lessons aimed at increasing emotional intelligence, social competence, and conflict-resolution skills. Social skills education has "improved outcomes related to drop out and attendance, grade retention, and special education referrals" (Smith 2010, 1). Furthermore, social skills curricula have been positively associated with improved student grades, test scores, and reading, math, and writing skills.

Transitional Kindergarten: An Extended Opportunity to Build a Strong Foundation for School Success

The goal of high-quality early education is to meet all learners where they are and support their development of new knowledge, skills, and abilities through integrated and differentiated instruction (Copple and Bredekamp 2009). As mentioned above, students enter TK with diverse early learning experiences. Some students may have attended preschool, while others may have remained at home—and in these different settings, it is likely that the children's exposure to rich language and cognitive experiences varied in terms of frequency and quality. As mentioned in chapter 1, the goal of high-quality transitional kindergarten is to bridge these variations in experiences and to provide extended opportunities for learning and socialization. TK students benefit from additional time, support, and experiences that prepare them to meet the challenges of a traditional kindergarten program in both social–emotional development and content-area instruction. A comprehensive approach that also addresses support for students with disabilities and English learners will be critical to ensure that high-quality education is provided for all students.

Students with Disabilities in the Transitional Kindergarten Classroom

"All students can benefit from high-quality experiences and may develop at different rates" (California County Superintendents Educational Services Association [CCSESA] 2011, 23). The TK classroom is intended as a place of learning for all students, including children with disabilities. As in the K–12 system, children with disabilities are included and educated with peers who do not have disabilities. Students receiving special education services may have participated in preschool programs prior to entrance into TK. For those students with an active IEP, transition requirements from preschool to TK will be followed and documented through an IEP team meeting.

Prior to enrollment in the TK classroom, the TK teacher attends the Transition/IEP meeting to gather as much information about the student. The IEP will contain information about the student's learning goals, his or her assessed strengths and needs, how the student will access the core curriculum, whether assistive technology supports are needed, and specialized instruction and services.

Students with disabilities receive instruction in the TK classroom that is specifically aligned with and supportive of the student's IEP. The teacher works collaboratively with a multi-disciplinary team that includes both special and general education staff to identify necessary additional support, set appropriate goals, monitor and adjust instruction, and evaluate individual progress. The instruction provided in the TK classroom facilitates each student's access to the curriculum, promotes the social–emotional development that supports and complements learning, and encourages engagement in all learning opportunities. Each child brings a unique set of characteristics and learning style to the classroom. A child with a diagnosed disability may manifest disability-specific characteristics requiring targeted classroom modifications and teaching supports that take into consideration a child's attention span, temperament, social skills, physical development, and communication skills. For instance, a child with cerebral palsy or spina bifida with physical–motor challenges may require alterations to room arrangement, seating, and positioning. An occupational therapist may be consulted to obtain recommendations on specific equipment, materials, and adjustments to the existing furniture and room organization. The changes will ensure the student has access to learning areas and classroom routines. A physical therapist may provide additional information on the child's physical capabilities and performance. Another example of disability specific characteristics is a child with Down syndrome. Although the student may be chronologically TK age, the student's skill development trajectory may benefit from additional reinforcement and repetition of concepts to achieve acquisition of grade-level skills.

A variety of specialized personnel can be called upon to provide consultation and support services for children with IEPs. A special education teacher may offer ways to simplify learning tasks and enhance them with added manipulatives and visual cues. The school psychologist can help develop behavioral support plans when the child requires support to follow classroom rules and routines. Children who exhibit limited vocabulary development may express themselves through nonverbal means such as pointing and gesturing. Sometimes, nonverbal communication may be disruptive and inappropriate—for example, hitting to get someone's attention. A speech–language pathologist possesses techniques for enhancing communication development during classroom activities and might provide direct service in the TK classroom to support both articulation skills and language development. Augmentative and alternative communication (AAC) devices may be provided as an enhancement to support the child's developing communication skills. Children with visual impairments need visual supports such as enlarged text on boards and books. Orientation and mobility specialists and visual impairment teachers on staff can be called upon to strategize the need for adaptations to enlarge print and adjust the room arrangement for ease of movement. Students who are deaf or hard of hearing (DHH) may need sign language interpreters, sound amplification systems, or minimization of extraneous noise. A DHH teacher may have additional ideas for the TK teacher to adopt in the classroom when a child with a hearing problem is identified. A child with autism may have difficulty with classroom transitions. A special educator can provide some examples of verbal, auditory and written cues to ease the movement from one activity to the next. Along with the cleanup song, the child might be offered a visual schedule of what comes next and a countdown timer to help understand the concept of time left in each activity.

Understanding child characteristics and obtaining information about how particular differences in temperament and sensory processing affect behavior and learning are paramount to implementing effective classroom adaptations. Additional suggestions and strategies for supporting students with special needs are provided in

chapter 4. TK students may also be identified as part of the ongoing assessment of foundational skills monitored in the TK classroom. If the TK teacher has a concern about a child in the classroom, the process for consultation and referral is initiated by the school district in which the TK program is operating. For further information, TK teachers can ask their site administrators about the referral process at their school site. The purpose of the referral is to explore the need for more in-depth testing and observation to confirm the child's eligibility for special education and related services. When the student qualifies for additional services under IDEA provisions, the IEP team will determine specific strategies for supporting the child in the TK classroom.

Students Who Are English Learners in the Transitional Kindergarten Classroom

Achieving academic success in school includes developing a knowledge and mastery of formal schooling practices in addition to building on one's home or community language practices. All children can have high levels of achievement if provided with a rich, challenging curriculum and appropriate forms of assistance (CDE 2009b, 4).

A TK classroom structure and environment that promotes and reinforces social interaction and engagement provides a strong foundation on which to build and extend second language skills. Providing strong oral language instruction and scaffolding with opportunities for social interaction and engagement is the cornerstone for both social–emotional development and academic growth. Opportunities for students to acquire early reading and writing skills can reflect attention to both the students' developmental levels and their need for explicit instruction. The California Department of Education has described 10 principles for promoting language, literacy, and learning that provide a foundation to effectively support preschool English learners (CDE 2009b). These principles provide guidance and direction for TK programs and are reflected throughout this

Principles for Promoting Language, Literacy, and Learning for Preschool English Learners (CDE 2009b, 91)

- The education of English learners is enhanced when preschool programs and families form meaningful partnerships.

- Children benefit when their teachers understand cultural differences in language use and incorporate them into the daily routine.

- Successful practices promote shared experiences in which language is used as a meaningful tool to communicate interests, ideas, and emotions.

- Language development and learning are promoted when preschool teachers and children creatively and interactively use language.

- Experimenting with the use, form, purpose, and intent of the first and second languages leads to growth in acquiring the second language.

- Continued use and development of the child's home language will benefit the child as he or she acquires English.

- Code switching is a normal part of language development for many bilingual children.

- Coordination and collaboration among families, teachers, and specialists become crucial in supporting the language and literacy development of children with disabilities and other special needs.

- Engaging in multiple literacy practices, such as reading books, singing songs, and reciting poetry, is part of the daily life of many families.

- Offering a variety of opportunities for children to explore written materials and their meanings as well as the sounds of spoken language through rhyme and alliteration builds the language and literacy skills of preschool English learners.

document. Specific suggestions and strategies for supporting English learners are provided in chapter 4.

Preparing the Transitional Kindergarten Student for Kindergarten

Although students enter the TK classroom with diverse backgrounds and unique strengths and needs, it is the goal of the program to prepare each student to successfully meet or exceed the challenging standards of California's kindergarten program as specified in California's Common Core State Standards for English language arts and mathematics, and the Content Standards for California Public Schools at the conclusion of their kindergarten year.

A modified kindergarten curriculum provided in a TK classroom will enable the student to transition into the traditional kindergarten program seamlessly and confidently. Modifications to ensure that TK students have extended opportunities to meet or exceed standards in traditional kindergarten are discussed in greater depth in the chapters cited below. These may include:

- adjusting the pace and intensity of instruction and slowing the release of responsibility to students (chapter 6);

- providing additional concrete experiences (chapter 6);

- providing additional scaffolding (chapter 6);

- reinforcing curricular connections through high-quality integration (chapter 3);

- increasing attention to the development of oral language and vocabulary skills (chapter 4).

While providing appropriate modifications and extended opportunities for their TK students, teachers should ensure that the TK program supports social–emotional development and remains focused on exposure to kindergarten standards in language arts, mathematics, science, history–social science, physical education, and visual/performing arts for success in traditional kindergarten and beyond.

Summary

TK students are unique in their developmental and experiential backgrounds. Although TK classes are typically composed of a chronologically similar age group, teachers recognize the students' unique needs and carefully plan and deliver an effective and developmentally appropriate educational program. Students entering the TK classroom will need high-quality instruction and support to develop social and emotional competence and to successfully achieve the rigorous academic standards they will encounter in their second year of kindergarten.

CHAPTER 3
Curriculum in a Transitional Kindergarten Program

Curriculum in a Transitional Kindergarten Program
http://www4.scoe.net/ims/webcasts/cf/index.
cfm?fuseaction=archivedDetail&eventID=140&archiveID=252

Curriculum in a Transitional Kindergarten Program (YouTube with Captions)
http://www.youtube.com/watch?v=8Ah23qle7_k

Transitional kindergarten (TK) teachers have a unique opportunity. They plan and implement a curriculum reflective of a developmental continuum. This continuum reinforces and builds upon preschool learning expectations to prepare students to meet or exceed rigorous standards at the completion of their second year of kindergarten. Senate Bill 1381 requires district to provide a "modified kindergarten curriculum that is age and developmentally appropriate" (*Education Code* Section 48000). As TK teachers conceptualize and plan the year in curriculum, they might consider these questions:

- Does my planned curriculum provide opportunities to actively engage students and emphasize experiential learning?

- Does my planned curriculum address the developmental needs of students?

- Does my planned curriculum provide a clear path that ensures exposure to kindergarten standards and builds a strong foundation for success?

The Alignment of the California Preschool Learning Foundations with Key Early Education Resources: California Infant/Toddler Learning and Development Foundations, California Content Standards,

Common Core State Standards, and Head Start Child Development and Early Learning Framework (CDE 2012c), referred to hereafter as the alignment document, provides critical information that assists teachers in their planning and supports other support staff involved in TK curriculum design. The first section of this chapter focuses on these curricular content resources and provides an overview of the TK curriculum components. The second section describes developmentally appropriate curriculum and effective curriculum integration. Guidelines for selecting and modifying the curriculum materials throughout the TK year are also reviewed.

The Transitional Kindergarten Curriculum

The California Preschool Learning Foundations (CDE 2008, CDE 2010b, and CDE 2013b), California's Common Core State Standards for kindergarten, and the kindergarten Content Standards for California Public Schools are resources that help teachers define what to teach in the TK classroom. Implementing a high-quality TK program requires a deep understanding of standards, as well as

Vignette

Mrs. Safier sits at her desk preparing her TK lesson plans for the following school week. She has a variety of resources, including the CDE alignment document, on her desk to support her work. Mrs. Safier's school district is modifying the kindergarten curriculum guides for TK. She reviews the lesson plans and then reflects on the current needs of her TK students. Mrs. Safier refers to the alignment document as she conceptualizes the adapted lesson plan. She plans to make minor changes to the general units that are outlined in the curriculum binders as discussed earlier at TK/K grade-level meetings. The concepts of focus will remain the same, but the selection of curriculum materials will be differentiated based on student background, their current assessed needs, interests, and areas of inquiry. She is confident that her revised and tailored lesson plan will meet the needs of her diverse TK learners. After the lesson, she will reflect on her observations and the information she gathered during instruction to ensure that her choice of curriculum materials targeted the students' needs and had the desired impact on student learning. Mrs. Safier will then determine whether to move forward or if a review of the concepts is needed.

extensive knowledge of child development and instructional strategies (Heroman and Copple 2006). Standards for learning provide an important structure for professional work. They serve as a map for selecting curriculum and support teachers as they guide students through diverse learning paths. Knowing what students need to learn and how they acquire knowledge and skills assists teachers in providing developmentally appropriate instruction. As TK teachers plan lessons, they recognize the value of incorporating a variety of instructional practices (e.g., single-concept/single skill approach, unit/theme approach, and project-based approach) to best fit conceptual development and stages of acquisition. Learning experiences should be meaningful and integrated across subject areas. Learning should also include experiential and hands-on activities in real contexts.

The CDE alignment document further illuminates the developmental and educational trajectories across infancy, early childhood, and elementary/school-age. Comparisons are made across the *California Infant/Toddler Learning and Development Foundations* (CDE 2009a), the California Preschool Learning Foundations (CDE 2008, CDE 2010b, and CDE 2013b), California's Common Core State Standards for kindergarten, and the Content Standards for California Public Schools (kindergarten). Having a deep knowledge of both preschool-age children and kindergartners is important for TK teachers who seek to differentiate and individualize instruction to meet the unique educational and social–emotional learning needs across the continuum of development (see figure 1).

Figure 1: Continuum of Development

Preschool
Foundational Learning Experiences

Individualize and Differentiate

Transitional Kindergarten
Exposure to the Common Core and Content Standards

Kindergarten
Mastery of the Common Core and Content Standards

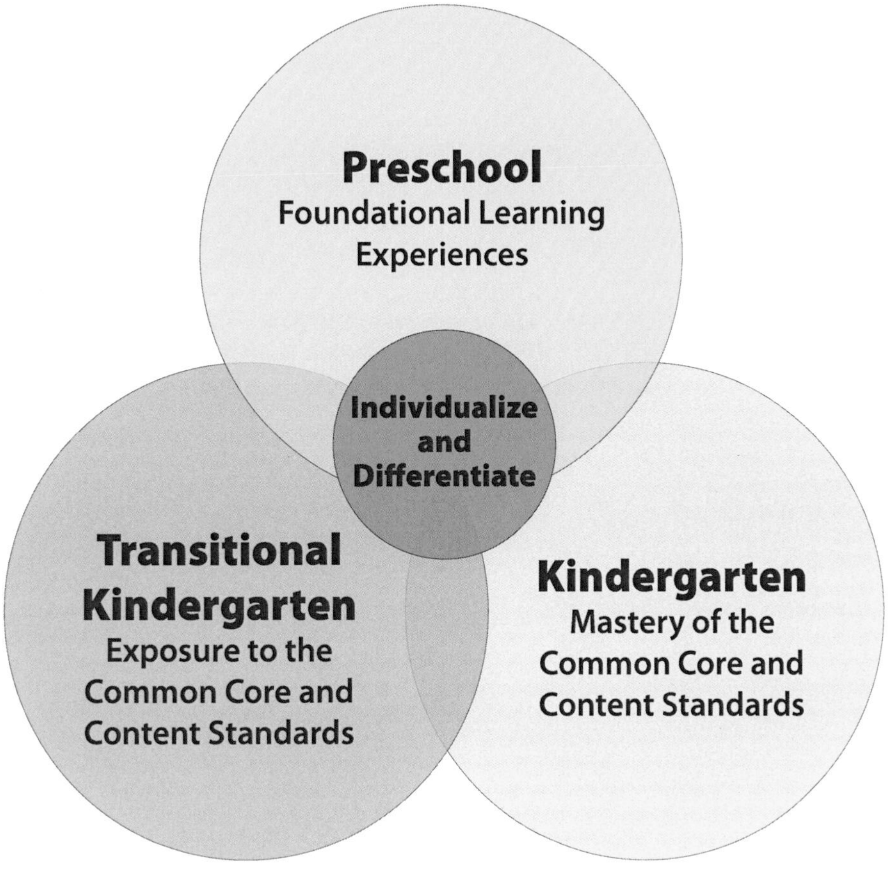

The California Preschool Learning Foundations—A Map for Instruction

The California Preschool Learning Foundations (CDE 2008, CDE 2010b, and CDE 2013b) introduce educators, administrators, specialists, policymakers, and families to children's development at 48 months and 60 months of age. The wide range of knowledge and skills described in this three-volume work reflect what children would typically accomplish when they have participated in a high-quality preschool program or comparable educational setting. The foundations serve as a map and a tool for monitoring children's development over time; TK teachers can reflect on where students are, where they have been, and where they are going. The specific content of the foundations is broken down as follows:

- Volume 1 (CDE 2008): Social–Emotional Development, Language and Literacy, English Language Development, and Mathematics
- Volume 2 (CDE 2010b): Visual and Performing Arts, Physical Development, and Health
- Volume 3 (CDE 2013b): History–Social Science and Science

Since TK students enter school with diverse backgrounds and early experiences, the California Preschool Learning Foundations will be useful at the beginning of the year as teachers seek to identify student knowledge and abilities. Foundations are a resource to understand children's development in the early years. TK teachers can use this resource to carefully observe their students for evidence of their current skills and conceptual understanding. Some students may be more or less advanced developmentally than what may be perceived for their actual age. Once a clear picture of individual and group development has been established, TK teachers can use the alignment document described below to design sequenced curriculum to meet the current needs and anticipate and plan for anticipated growth and learning.

As TK teachers make decisions about what to teach and seek to distinguish their programs from those of preschool and kindergarten, the CDE alignment

Using the CDE Alignment Document

The CDE alignment document (CDE 2012c) is organized into three main segments: *Introduction, Section 1: Alignment of the California Infant/Toddler Learning and Development Foundations, Preschool Learning Foundations, and Kindergarten Content Standards for Each Domain*, and *Section 2: Alignment Between the California Preschool Learning Foundations and the Head Start Child Development Early Learning Framework*. The introduction provides the reader with the context for the development of foundations and standards and offers a brief description of the organization of each early learning resource. Additionally, the introduction highlights key characteristics of early development and learning. A table is presented to illustrate the alignment of foundations across domains of development (e.g., social–emotional development or language and literacy). The subsequent segments, section 1 and section 2, provide concise summaries of the developmental progression of key preschool foundations in each domain as they relate to specific infant/toddler foundations, specific Common Core State Standards, specific kindergarten content standards, and specific competencies as described in the *Head Start Learning Framework*. A TK teacher may use the alignment document to acquire a deeper understanding of children's development over time and to plan curriculum that spans a continuum of learning. The following example demonstrates the possible use of the CDE alignment document in TK curriculum planning:

It is the beginning of the school year. Miss Garcia is preparing a writing lesson for her TK students to match her current curricular focus: travel. To inform her work, she turns to page 62 in the CDE alignment document. She reviews the content related to emergent writing skills at around 48 months, 60 months, and by the end of kindergarten.

1. She notes that some students in her TK class may be at the emergent level, experimenting with grasp and scribbling, while others are developing increased control and writing letters or letter-like shapes to represent words or ideas. She also notes that some students may be prepared to explore the Common Core kindergarten standards related to proper letter formation and/or writing phonetically spelled words. Miss Garcia then compares the content with what she has observed in her TK classroom. She sees a great deal of variability in her students fine-motor control and letter writing ability; some students show confidence and competence in their ability to hold a pencil and write their name, while others seem less comfortable in their work.

2. Miss Garcia reflects on her goals for learning and checks that they match appropriate standards for learning. She determines that she will support the students' learning through the following activities, which encourage specific skills:

   a. Take classroom attendance by reading aloud student name cards and running her finger across print to build familiarity with letter names, letter shapes, and print concepts (e.g., moving left to right).

   b. Build fine-motor control by offering different writing instruments and adjustable grips throughout the classroom environment.

   c. Draw attention to directionality by guiding students to "write" their name in the Language and Literacy Area using magnet letters and other letter manipulatives. Have picture cards with each student's image and blank lines for filling in letters.

   d. Prompt students to practice name writing by providing blank luggage tags in the Dramatic Play Area airport. Post a list of student names near the "check-in" desk.

document provides a framework for planning. After familiarizing themselves with the structure and content, TK teachers can use the document to plan the beginning, middle and end of the school year. The alignment document also provides guidance for teachers as they reflect on the assessed needs of their students and work to plan the differentiated instruction that will either support students' readiness for their next learning challenge or their need for additional support, or provide additional practice or review related to their current goal.

Transitional Kindergarten Curriculum Content: Bridging Preschool and Kindergarten

The following areas include the foundational content of TK curriculum.

Social–Emotional Development

A focal point of the TK year is social–emotional development. Students learn to identify and regulate emotions, establish and sustain their relationships with others, and work in collaboration to achieve program goals. Some concepts for instruction are as follows (CCSESA 2011; CDE 2012c):

- Developing and maintaining a positive sense of self and rewarding relationships with others, including adults and peers

- Identifying emotions in themselves and managing their impulses and emotions

- Following rules and meeting expectations

- Learning to work in both independent and cooperative situations

- Focusing attention

- Initiating and sustaining peer play

- Resolving social conflict

English Language Arts

TK students are growing in their ability to communicate with others, express ideas, and reason using language. They are beginning to represent thoughts and ideas using written symbols. Their ability to attend to a variety of texts including both literary (e.g., comprehend characters, setting, sequence of events) and expository texts (e.g., comprehend, sequence, identify facts) is also developing. A balance of explicit instruction and student-initiated learning is important to exposing children to standards-based instruction. The following list merges information from the substrands of the California Preschool Learning Foundations and the strands of the Common Core standards to provide an overview of the English language arts curriculum.

- Early listening and speaking opportunities focused on vocabulary and grammar build a foundation for kindergarten standards related to comprehension and collaboration, presentation of knowledge, vocabulary acquisition and demonstration of the conventions of standard English.

- Early vocabulary activities focused on understanding and using an increasing variety and specificity of words, categories, and both simple and complex words that describe relations between objects build a foundation for kindergarten skills related to determining and clarifying the meaning of unknown words, exploring word relationships, and using acquired words and phrases in speech and writing.

- Early phonological awareness activities focused on oral blending and deleting words and syllables, onsets, rimes and phonemes build a foundation for kindergarten phonological awareness standards related to understanding spoken words and manipulating syllables, and sounds.

- Early concepts about print activities focused on appropriate book handling, knowledge of print conventions, and understanding that print carries meaning build a foundation for kindergarten standards focused on understanding the organization and basic features of print and the craft and structure of literature and informational text.

- Early alphabetics and word/print recognition activities focused on recognizing students' names and common words in print, matching letter names to their printed forms, and beginning to recognize that letters have sounds build a foundation for recognizing and naming all upper and lowercase letters of the alphabet and understanding kindergarten phonics and word recognition standards.

- Early opportunities for and guidance in demonstrating comprehension and analysis of details in a familiar story and of information from informational text build a foundation for kindergarten literature and informational text standards (e.g., key details and ideas, integration of knowledge and ideas, comprehension and collaboration).

- Early opportunities for and guidance in developing increased control in writing and drawing, writing letter or letter-like shapes to represent words or ideas, and writing the first name correctly build a foundation for kindergarten skills related to drawing, dictating, and writing to compose opinion pieces, informative/explanatory texts, and narration of a single event.

Mathematics

Teachers in the TK year assist students as they move from intuitive, every day mathematics to mathematics taught in school. In addition to highlighting math skills such as number sense and measurement, TK teachers support the development of mathematical reasoning (e.g., representing, relating, analyzing, and explaining). Instruction on the following can help prepare students for meeting the Common Core standards by the end of kindergarten (CDE 2012c):

- Early opportunities to recite numbers to 20, recognize and name some numerals, count up to 10 objects, and understand that the number name of the last object counted represents the total number, build a foundation for kindergarten skills such as counting to 100, writing numbers from 0 to 20, one-to-one correspondence, responding to "how many?" by the end of kindergarten.

- Early activities related to comparing groups, understanding that adding or subtracting one changes the number, combining two groups to make a larger group (and vice versa), and to solving simple addition and subtraction problems support children as they work with "greater than," "less than," and "equal to" represent addition and subtraction in a variety of ways, decompose numbers less than or equal to 10, find the number that makes 10 when added to any number 1–9, and fluently add and subtract within 5 in kindergarten.

- Early opportunities to sort and classify objects, recognize and duplicate patterns, and extend and create patterns build a foundation for kindergarten skills such as classifying objects, counting objects in a category, and sorting categories by the count.

- Early opportunities to compare the length, weight, or capacity of objects, order four or more objects by size, and measure length prepare students to describe measurable attributes of objects, and directly compare two objects with a measurable attribute in common to see which has "more of" or "less of" the attribute in kindergarten.

- Early activities related to identifying, describing, and constructing a variety of shapes and combining shapes to create a picture design prepare kindergarten students to describe objects in the environment using names of shapes, correctly name shapes regardless of size or orientation, identify shapes as two- or three-dimensional, analyze and compare two- and three-dimensional shapes, build and draw shapes, and compose simple shapes to form larger shapes.

- Early experiences in identifying the position of objects and people in space enable kindergarten students to describe the relative positions of objects.

Science

Young learners are naturally curious. Science learning in the TK classroom focuses on teaching inquiry skills through the use of simple science equipment and books (CCSESA 2011; Jacobs and Crowley 2010). Experiences that explore the diverse areas of scientific study (e.g., physical science, life science, earth science) can be integrated into other subjects including English language arts, mathematics, history–social science, physical education, and visual and performing arts. Many of the preschool foundation skills listed below require teacher instruction and guidance as TK students prepare to successfully meet or exceed California's kindergarten content standards. Instruction should focus on the following elements (CDE 2012c):

- Early opportunities to demonstrate curiosity and raise questions, observe and describe objects and events in the environment, identify and use a variety of observational tools, compare and contrast objects, make and check predictions, and demonstrate increased ability to make inferences enable kindergarten students to ask meaningful questions and conduct careful investigations using five senses to observe, describe and compare and sort. At this level, the Investigation and Experimentation strand is also aligned with mathematics skills and concepts.

- Early activities involving recording information in a variety of ways and sharing findings prepare children to communicate observations, pose questions, collect data, and record data in kindergarten.

- Early opportunities to observe, investigate, and describe characteristics and physical properties of objects and materials enable kindergarten students to know that objects can be described in terms of the materials they are made of and their physical properties (e.g., shape texture, flexibility, and the like).

- Early activities to develop an increased awareness that objects and materials can change, and an increased ability to observe and to describe in greater detail provide the foundation for understanding that water can be a liquid or solid and can change from one form to the other, and that water left in an open container evaporates.

- Early opportunities to identify characteristics of animals and plants, demonstrate an increased ability to categorize animals and plants, and demonstrate greater knowledge of body parts and processes in humans and other animals enable kindergarten students to observe and describe similarities and differences in plants and animals and to identify major structures of common plants and animals.

- Early opportunities to investigate and compare characteristics of earth materials, such as sand and rocks, lay the foundation for the kindergarten standard related to knowing the characteristics of mountains, rivers, and oceans.

- Early experiences to observe, describe, and discuss changes in weather and describe the effects of weather on their own lives and on plants and animals prepare children to understand that changes in weather affect the earth and its inhabitants on a daily basis and across seasons.

History–Social Science

Exploring history–social science in the TK years begins with students learning about themselves, their families, and their local communities. Language, family, and culture are important topics for consideration as teachers work to make curriculum meaningful and relevant (CCSESA 2011). Student knowledge can be extended to include time, space, and social connections (Seefeldt and

Galper 2006). Instruction may focus on the skills listed below. Many of the preschool foundation skills listed require teacher instruction and guidance as TK students prepare to successfully meet or exceed California's kindergarten content standards (CDE 2012):

- Early experiences that encourage children to demonstrate their cultural, ethnic, and racial identity and show interest in diversity support kindergarten students' recognition of national and state symbols and icons.

- Early opportunities to understand the mutual responsibilities of relationships and to take initiative in developing relationships enable children to follow rules, such as sharing and taking turns, and to understand the consequences of breaking them.

- Early opportunities to exhibit understanding of a variety of adult roles and occupations provide the foundation for matching descriptions of the work people do and the names of related jobs in kindergarten.

- Early opportunities for children to become involved in group activities (e.g., including decision making, respect for the majority, and valuing views of others), to exhibit responsible conduct, to pay attention to others' feelings, and to negotiate and compromise prepare them to follow rules and learn about American and world history examples of honesty, courage, determination, for example, from stories and folklore.

- Early opportunities to develop an interest in family history enable kindergarten children to understand that history relates to events, people, and places of other times, to identify the purposes of holidays, to understand the triumphs of American legends, and to understand how people lived in earlier times.

- Early activities that encourage children to create drawings, maps, and models and to use globes enable children to distinguish between land and water on maps, identify traffic

symbols, and construct maps and models of neighborhoods in kindergarten.

Physical Education

Instruction in physical education supports healthy growth and motor skill development, and has an impact on the developing brain. Many of the preschool foundational skills listed below require teacher instruction and guidance as TK students prepare to successfully meet or exceed California's kindergarten content standards. Among the many skills listed in the alignment document, instruction might focus on the following (CDE 2012c):

- Early experiences that promote increasing balance and control while still and while moving enable kindergarten children to create shapes using various body parts and by using nonlocomotor movements; to balance on one, two, three, four, and five body parts; and to balance while walking forward and sideways on a narrow, elevated surface.

- Early experiences that encourage children to walk with balance and oppositional arm movement enable kindergarten children to balance while walking forward and sideways on a narrow, elevated surface and identify locomotor skills of walk, jog, run, hop, and so on.

- Early experiences that encourage children to run with a longer stride for a greater length of time enable kindergarten children to travel in straight, curved, and zigzag paths.

- Early experiences that encourage children to jump for height and distance enable kindergarten children to jump over a stationary rope and identify the locomotor skills.

- Early experiences that allow children to practice gross-motor manipulative skills by using arms, hands, and feet (e.g., rolling, tossing, or bouncing a ball) enable kindergarten children to strike a stationary ball, toss a ball, kick a stationary object, and bounce a ball continuously.

- Early activities that increase children's knowledge of body parts enable kindergarten children to identify and describe parts of the body.

- Early experiences that allow children to use their own body and general space, for example, enable kindergarten children to travel within a large group without bumping into others or falling and to identify and use personal space, general space, and boundaries.

Visual and Performing Arts

TK students should have opportunities to explore creative expression in the following areas: dance, music, theater, and visual arts (CCSESA 2011). Educators can support art appreciation skills, helping children to focus on unique aspects of artwork, reflecting on aesthetic choices, and recognizing the feelings that are creatively expressed (Epstein 2007, 118–119). Many of the preschool foundation skills listed below require teacher instruction and guidance as TK students prepare to successfully meet or exceed California's kindergarten content standards. Among the many skills listed in the alignment document, instruction might focus on the following (CDE 2012):

- Early activities that increase children's ability to plan art and show increasing care and persistence enable kindergarten children to discuss their own works of art, using appropriate art vocabulary.

- Early activities that encourage children to choose their own art for display or for inclusion in a portfolio or book and explain their ideas enable kindergarten children to discuss how and why they make a specific work of art and give reasons why they like it.

- Early activities that increase children's ability to begin to intentionally create representative paintings or drawings that approximate or depict people, animals, and objects enable kindergarten children to paint pictures expressing ideas about family and

neighborhood and use lines in drawings and paintings to express feelings.

- Early activities that increase children's ability to demonstrate increasing coordination and motor control when working with visual art tools enable kindergarten children to demonstrate beginning skill in the use of tools and processes, such as the use of scissors, glue, and paper in creating three-dimensional construction.

- Early activities that encourage children to verbally reflect on music and describe music using an expanded vocabulary enable kindergarten children to identify and describe basic elements in music such as high/low, fast/slow, loud/soft, and beat.

- Early activities that encourage children to use body movement to respond to beat, dynamics, and tempo enable kindergarten children to create movements that correspond to specific music.

- Early activities that encourage children to demonstrate extended role play skills with increased imagination and creativity enable kindergarten children to perform imitative movements, rhythmical activities, and theater games such as freeze, statues, and mirrors.

- Early activities that encourage children to invent and recreate dance movements enable kindergarten children to create movements that reflect a variety of personal experiences, to respond to a variety of stimuli (e.g., sounds, words, songs) with original movements.

Integrated Transitional Kindergarten Curriculum

Conceptual development does not occur in isolation of other knowledge. Students learn best when teachers promote meaningful connections across subject matter and involve learners in integrated educational experiences. TK teachers who integrate curricular content in meaningful ways promote active learning and exploration and reinforce critical connections between what is known and new knowledge. "Teachers integrate ideas and content from multiple domains and disciplines through themes, projects, play opportunities, and other learning experiences so that children are able to develop an understanding of concepts and make connections across content areas" (Copple and Bredekamp 2009, 161). The authors contrast this type of meaningful and purposeful integration with integration that is fragmented and fails to connect curriculum topics in ways that are meaningful to children (see figure 2).

Integrated instruction begins with the teacher deciding on a connecting thread and generating a lesson plan based on the interdisciplinary area

Figure 2: Integrated Instruction

- Learning areas offer multiple points of entry, both indoors and outdoors, for exploring concepts and skills
- Curriculum is designed to work across subject matter
- Materials are displayed with intentionality to promote conceptual learning

Environment

Integrated Instruction

- Interactive study in individual, small-group, or whole-group learning experiences
- A broad range of strategies are used to determine what students know and can do, and their knowledge about processes used to solve real-world problems

Instruction

Assessment

- Organized to make meaningful, real-world connections
- Students are observed in different contexts throughout the daily routine
- Exploring concepts over time
- Teachers utilize data from independent explorations as well as collaborative work with peers and adults

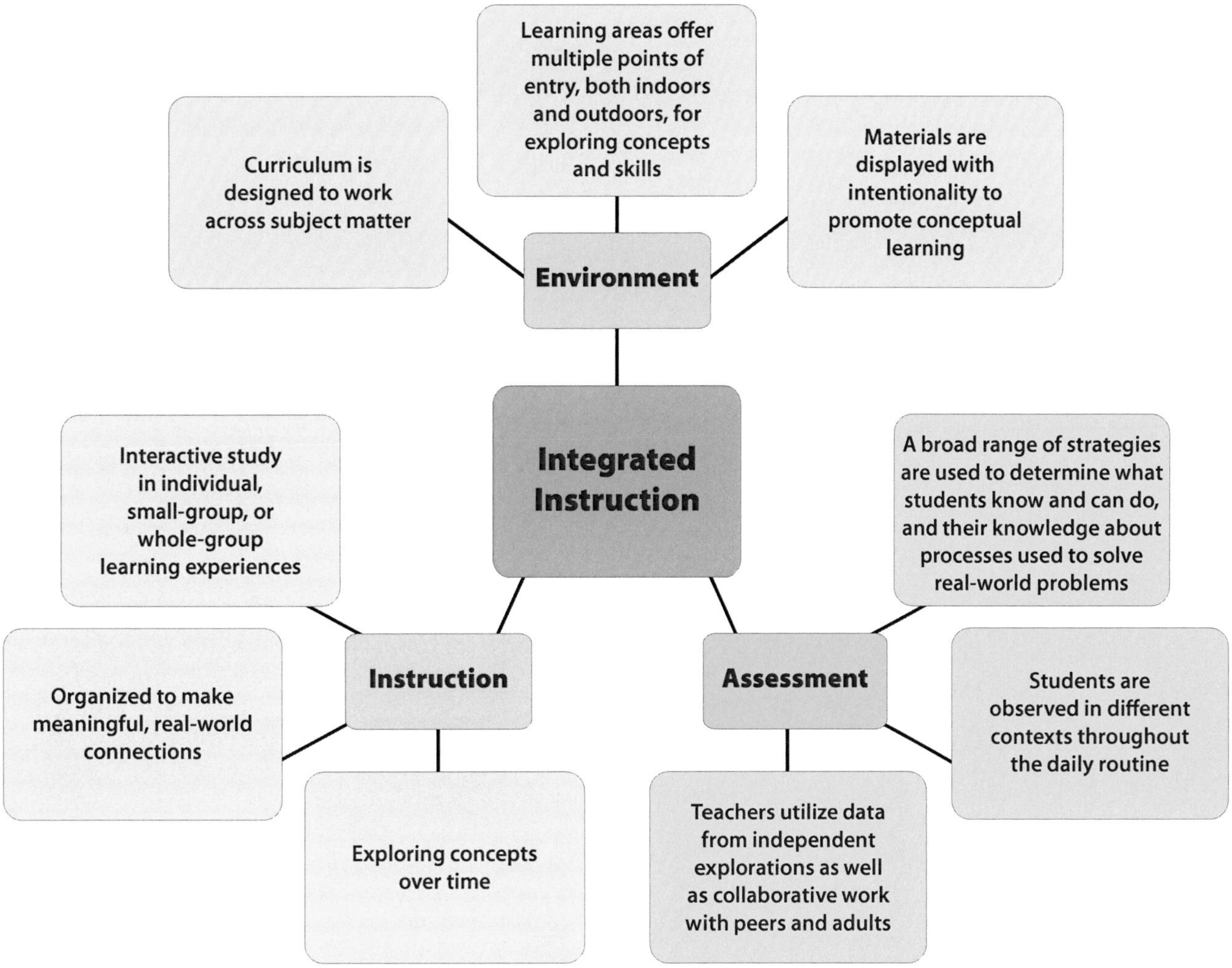

Vignette

It was a sunny Monday morning after a spring storm. During the previous weeks, the students in Miss Pires' class developed an interest in worms that were found in the school play yard. Knowing that the students would be exploring measurement, Miss Pires adapted her lesson plan to include an integrated learning experience. She collected inch blocks, rulers, clipboards, pencils, orange cones, and shovels in preparation for this experience. At the morning meeting, Miss Pires introduced the book Diary of a Worm to set the stage for the small-group project. She read portions of the book and then explained the next steps. "Today we are putting on our scientist hats. We are going outside to dig for worms in our play yard. You are going to find a work zone (designated by orange cones), and with a buddy you are going to draw and measure the worms you find." Miss Pires reinforced her instructions by drawing, labeling, and repeating the steps; first drawing an orange cone, then showing inch blocks and rulers, and then introducing the tools for documenting the work. She then modeled the use of the measuring tools with the help of a few students. Miss Pires then organized the students into pairs and led them outdoors. While the students worked, Miss Pires moved around offering individualized assistance to the different groups of learners. Before bringing the activity to a close, Miss Pires took note of the student conversations, paying careful attention to additional areas of inquiry and potential future projects based on the group's ongoing interest in worms. Miss Pires is pleased that she has been able to successfully integrate English language arts, mathematics, and science into engaging learning experiences that will set the stage for success in traditional kindergarten and beyond.

of study (see figure 3). In the case of the vignette, the common thread was the study of worms. Broad themes, such as learning about community heroes or exploring structures, naturally lend themselves to integrated learning experiences. Students are especially invested in learning themes when they are developed from their own purposeful play and questions for study. Once an area of focus has been determined, TK teachers can generate both student-initiated encounters as well as teacher-directed learning experiences that expand students' learning. Teachers may find it useful to create a web to plan the project theme, activities, and connections to the California Preschool Learning Foundations, California's Common Core State Standards for kindergarten, and the kindergarten Content Standards for California Public Schools. A large-group meeting is an ideal time to introduce the integrated project. A short story or a "picture walk" can do much to lay the foundation for the upcoming activity and

Figure 3: Integrated Lesson Planning

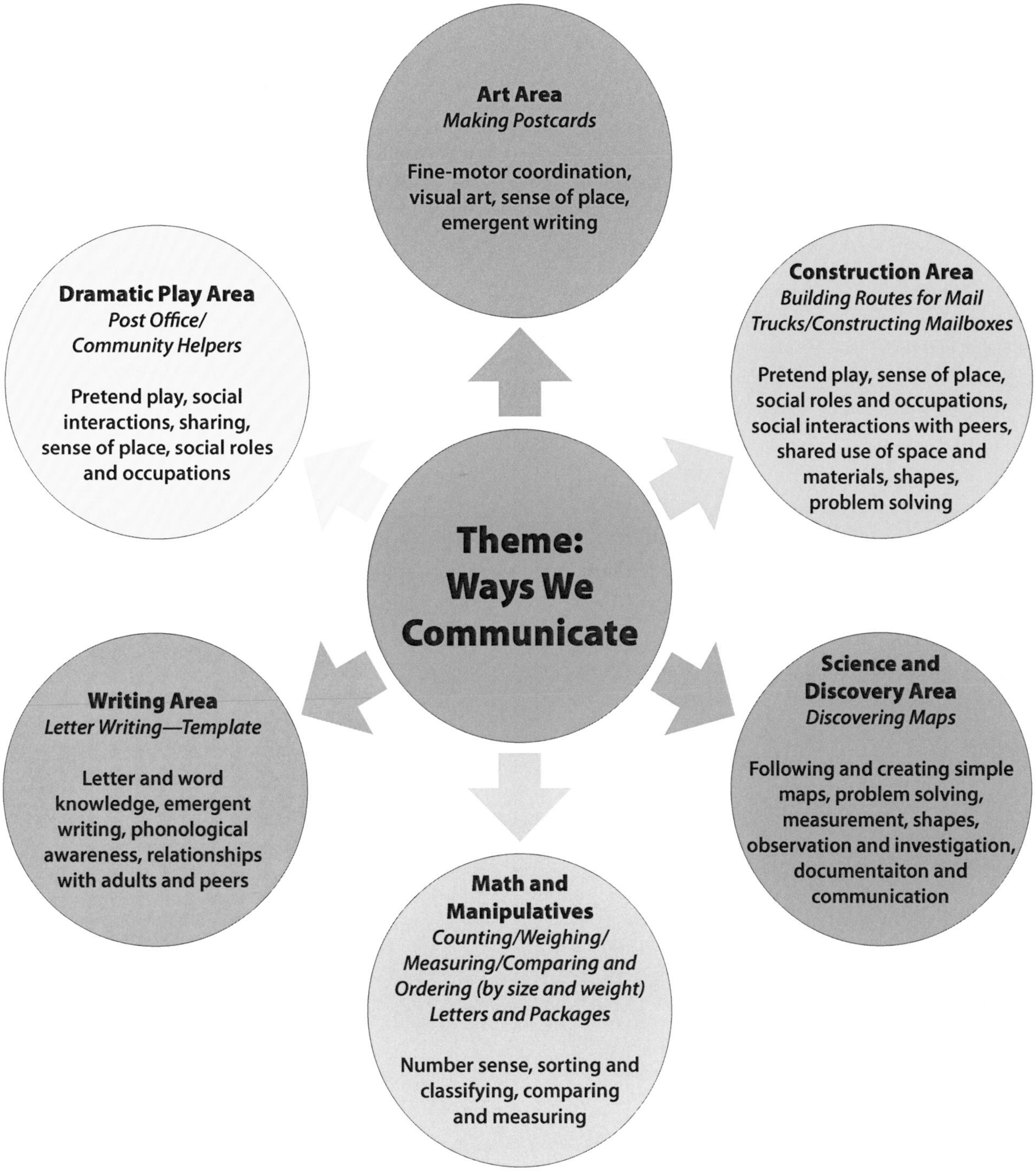

Theme: Ways We Communicate

Art Area
Making Postcards

Fine-motor coordination, visual art, sense of place, emergent writing

Dramatic Play Area
Post Office/ Community Helpers

Pretend play, social interactions, sharing, sense of place, social roles and occupations

Construction Area
Building Routes for Mail Trucks/Constructing Mailboxes

Pretend play, sense of place, social roles and occupations, social interactions with peers, shared use of space and materials, shapes, problem solving

Writing Area
Letter Writing—Template

Letter and word knowledge, emergent writing, phonological awareness, relationships with adults and peers

Science and Discovery Area
Discovering Maps

Following and creating simple maps, problem solving, measurement, shapes, observation and investigation, documentaiton and communication

Math and Manipulatives
Counting/Weighing/ Measuring/Comparing and Ordering (by size and weight) Letters and Packages

Number sense, sorting and classifying, comparing and measuring follow-up experiences throughout the classroom environment. Careful staging of materials within learning areas assists students as they revisit concepts and apply newly acquired knowledge to their student-initiated work.

Guidelines for Selecting and Modifying Curriculum Materials

Educators invested in sustaining student enthusiasm and active engagement rotate materials over time to meet emerging abilities and interests (Heroman and Copple 2006). TK teachers who incorporate a variety of experiences into the classroom reinforce conceptual learning. Effective teachers design challenging activities to introduce advanced knowledge and invite students into the learning process. To implement a modified kindergarten curriculum, teachers may make modifications to locally developed or commercially published curricula. Curriculum can be used as a "blueprint" for classroom decision making (Heroman and Copple 2006). TK teachers can walk themselves through a series of questions designed to adapt curriculum to meet individual and group learning needs. The following guidelines for reflection help educators decide what to teach and how to provide instruction:

- What standards am I focusing on in this lesson?

- How does the curriculum address these standards?

- How will I meet the individual needs of each student and assess progress?

- What adaptations do I need to make to the curriculum that will reflect student interests, backgrounds, and current areas of inquiry?

- Where might I integrate the learning across curricular areas, the learning environment, and daily routine?

TK teachers need to thoughtfully respond to each of these questions as they create curriculum plans that are meaningful and developmentally appropriate for their students.

Summary

Successful TK programs are the result of thoughtful teacher reflection and planning. The TK teacher has a thorough understanding of the TK curriculum and understands the critical skills and concepts for each subject area. TK teachers understand the developmental trajectories of their students and identify the standards for learning that align with both students' assessed needs and effective instructional strategies (see chapter 4). TK teachers create cohesive curriculum plans that are reflective of individual and group learning needs. Decisions about what to teach in a TK classroom are guided by key CDE resources, including the recently published alignment document. Guidelines for selecting and adapting curriculum materials and lessons help TK teachers plan engaging encounters that address learning standards.

CHAPTER 4
Effective Instruction in a Transitional Kindergarten Program

Effective Instruction in a Transitional Kindergarten Program
http://www4.scoe.net/ims/webcasts/cf/index.
cfm?fuseaction=archivedDetail&eventID=140&archiveID=253

Effective Instruction in a Transitional Kindergarten Program (YouTube with Captions)
http://www.youtube.com/watch?v=Qv7x2Up4HC8

The transitional kindergarten (TK) year strongly influences student expectations for school as well as their goals for lifelong learning. Class routines, activities, and experiences influence a student's level of enthusiasm and excitement for learning. TK teachers should be aware of the implicit and explicit messages they send to students in their program design and daily interactions. Reflecting on the educational experiences TK teachers provide for their students is central to instructional planning.

As discussed in chapter 3, TK teachers carefully plan and organize the curriculum for their students. When selecting an appropriate curriculum focus in a given area, TK teachers consider their students' backgrounds, reflect on their current developmental levels and assessed needs, and then carefully develop a plan toward established goals. TK teachers are intentional in this planning, "the intentional teacher . . . acts with knowledge and purpose to ensure that young children acquire the knowledge and skills (content) they need to succeed in school and in life. Intentional teaching does not happen by chance; it is planful, thoughtful, and purposeful. Intentional teachers use their knowledge, judgment, and expertise to organize learning experiences for children" (Epstein 2007, 1).

The TK teacher intentionally links thoughtful curriculum decisions with carefully selected instructional strategies and related activities that align with both the curriculum and the developmental needs of students. This chapter provides an overview of strategies that align with TK curriculum and, when applied with purposeful intent, provide students with highly effective instruction and a positive TK experience.

Using Knowledge of Child Development to Guide Instructional Strategy Decisions

Educators of young children are charged with facilitating the cognitive development of children while also building their understanding of the

Vignette

Mr. Wright has been reflecting on his students' progress in math. Based on his observations and informal assessments, he decides that most of his students need more opportunities to work with one-to-one correspondence and additional modeling and practice to understand that when counting objects, the number name of the last item counted represents the total number of objects in a group. As he plans his instruction for the following week, Mr. Wright knows he needs to carefully select activities that will align with his goals, so he decides to model counting familiar objects in the classroom during large-group instruction. He will begin by laying out 10 carpet squares, counting each one, and then asking, "How many are there altogether?" He will use a specific signal when he says "altogether" (bring his hands together to form a circle) to cue the appropriate response. He will then invite students to stand on each square, repeat the counting sequence, and ask how many altogether with the cue and repeat the process with different numbers as time and attention allows. He will engage the rest of the class by having them count on their fingers as students are counted and use the same "altogether" signal in response. To reinforce this lesson, Mr. Wright will circulate during free exploration and engage students in informal discussions that focus on one-to-one correspondence and on being able to state the total number of objects (e.g., "Let's count the number of blocks in your stack. Oh, there are 10 blocks altogether"). Students who count accurately and identify the total number confidently will have opportunities to build on their knowledge at the Math and Manipulatives Area.

routines and expectations of school. Young children's brains are still under construction, their vocabularies are expanding, their ability to attend to tasks and manage impulses is increasing, and the connections between concepts and experiences are fusing together to create knowledge. Children are also acquiring the important social skills needed for peer and adult–child relationships. Development is a complex, interwoven process (National Research Council and Institute of Medicine 2000). The skills and knowledge that are needed do not emerge in isolation; they influence and shape each other as they develop. In this section, a holistic approach to TK education with an emphasis on developmentally appropriate practice is discussed.

Knowledge of Child Development as a Foundation for Instruction

To provide TK students with quality education that supports all areas of development, educators should be knowledgeable about key aspects of cognitive, physical, social, and emotional development. A background in child development will assist TK teachers as they plan curriculum and related instructional strategies that are engaging and appropriately challenging. Teachers who understand the complexities of development are better able to observe students during learning experiences. Responsive teachers check for understanding, monitor children's progress, and individualize instruction to match the emerging needs of the learners (Ritchie, Maxwell, and Bredekamp 2009).

There are several resources to assist educators as they review and apply promising practices based on research in child development. The California Preschool Learning Foundations, created and published by the California Department of Education, highlights the progression of diverse skills and areas of learning for children at 40 and 60 months of age. Additional information can be found in the highlight titled "The California Preschool Learning Foundations—A Map for Instruction" in chapter 3. Another resource to promote appropriate

Vignette

Miss Sanchez observes Olivia working with a collection of small beads and yarn at the Art Area. She watches as Olivia carefully slides each bead onto the yarn before commenting, "Olivia, it looks like you are working hard on this project. Tell me about it." "It's for my mom. It's a necklace," replied Olivia. "How special! I think she will be excited to see the necklace you have made," reinforces Miss Sanchez. She pauses a moment as she recalls an earlier conversation with Olivia at arrival time. Miss Sanchez has an idea to extend Olivia's child-initiated play to further her writing skills. "I remember you telling me you had a special treat with your mom on your walk to school today for her birthday. It sounds like you two had a lot of fun," says Miss Sanchez. "I wonder if you would like to make a card to go along with your gift?" "I know 'M-O-M,' but I don't know how to write 'Happy Birthday,'" says Olivia softly. "I bet you could learn with a little help from our Language and Literacy Area word cards. I will get them for you and come back to get you started." "Okay," Olivia replies with a wide smile. A short time later, as Olivia makes progress on her writing, Miss Sanchez returns to provide descriptive feedback: "You are doing it! You have written 'Happy' and are almost finished with 'Birthday'! It looks like the word cards helped. I am proud of you, and you must be proud of yourself for writing such big words!"

expectations for educators and guidance for instruction is *Developmentally Appropriate Practice in Early Childhood Programs Serving Children from Birth Through Age 8* (Copple and Bredekamp 2009), a publication offered by the National Association for the Education of Young Children (NAEYC). This

Developmentally Appropriate Practice in Transitional Kindergarten Classrooms

As outlined in Section 48000 of the California *Education Code*, TK is the "first year of a two-year kindergarten program that uses a modified kindergarten curriculum that is age and developmentally appropriate." It is recommended that educators review and reflect on resources aimed to promote developmentally appropriate practice. *Developmentally Appropriate Practice in Early Childhood Programs Serving Children from Birth Through Age 8* (Copple and Bredekamp 2009) provides an introduction for teachers to offer TK students appropriately stimulating and challenging environments and instruction. The publication (Copple and Bredekamp 2009, 10–15) introduces the following principles of child development and learning to inform practice:

- All the domains of development—physical, social and emotional, and cognitive—are important, and they are closely interrelated. Children's development and learning in one domain influence and are influenced by what takes place in other domains.

- Many aspects of children's learning and development follow well-documented sequences, with later abilities, skills, and knowledge building on those already acquired.

- Development and learning proceed at varying rates from child to child, as well as at uneven rates across different areas of a child's individual functioning.

- Development and learning result from a dynamic and continuous interaction of biological maturation and experience.

- Early experiences have profound effects, both cumulative and delayed, on a child's development and learning; and optimal periods exist for certain types of development and learning to occur.

- Development proceeds toward greater complexity, self-regulation, and symbolic or representational capacities.

- Children develop best when they have secure, consistent relationships with responsive adults and opportunities for positive relationships with peers.

- Development and learning occur in and are influenced by multiple social and cultural contexts.

- Always mentally active in seeking to understand the world around them, children learn in a variety of ways; a wide range of teaching strategies and interactions are effective in supporting all these kinds of learning.

- Play is an important vehicle for developing self-regulation as well as for promoting language, cognition, and social competence.

- Development and learning advance when children are challenged to achieve at a level just beyond their current mastery, and when children have many opportunities to practice newly acquired skills.

- Children's experiences shape their motivation and approach to learning such as persistence, initiative, and flexibility; in turn, these dispositions and behaviors affect their learning and development.

publication expands the approach to meeting children's developmental and learning needs to include the consideration of culture, the individual, and the individual within a group of learners.

A Balanced Approach to Teaching and Learning

Integrated lessons in the TK classroom are most effectively conducted through a balanced approach that includes a wide variety of student-initiated, teacher-directed, and teacher-guided learning activities. As young learners work purposefully to explore their learning environment, they participate as active investigators in experiential and hands-on activities. Student-initiated work and exploration allow TK students to learn in a "hands-on" fashion (Jacobs and Crowley 2010). Explicit instruction is an effective tool for presenting ideas and skills, but it should be balanced with student-initiated opportunities. Young learners are dynamic explorers who benefit from intentional teaching that invites reflection, encourages repetition and practice, and reinforces critical thinking. TK students are "learning to learn"

(Heroman and Copple 2006, 62). They develop the skills and dispositions that foster school achievement such as independence, appropriate risk-taking, perseverance, initiative, creativity, reasoning, and problem solving.

As discussed above, active learning encourages discovery and promotes problem solving. When students are engaged in purposeful play, they are active learners and motivated participants in their learning environments. Through their senses, choices, and social interactions, students build their understanding of words and concepts and make meaningful connections across experiences and content areas. They work from familiar and meaningful themes to develop deep understandings of language, patterns, relationships, and other academic content (Heidemann and Hewitt 2010). Teachers who attend to the emerging interests of students and provide them with opportunities to explore, investigate, and review content standards tap into students' natural curiosity to further their learning and skill development.

The Developing Brain and Play-based Instruction in the Transitional Kindergarten Classroom

Active learning through purposeful play is important to the development of the child's brain. From birth, experiences shape the formation of neurons and synapses building important connections that influence language, cognitive, social–emotional, and physical development. Although some sections of the brain are fully formed in early childhood, others are still under construction well into adolescence (Copple 2012). One area that develops over time is the cerebral cortex. The cortex controls and regulates executive functions such as language, cognitive reasoning, and decision making. Developmentally, young children struggle with abstract lessons and instead show greater competencies and understanding in concrete, hands-on, learning contexts. Purposeful play that invites engagement, promotes peer interactions, and encourages problem solving provides the ideal framework for concrete learning while also setting the stage for future abstract, logical thinking. Educators who prompt students to make plans, implement ideas, and evaluate outcomes encourage young learners to express their intentions and reflect on their actions and discoveries (Hohmann, Weikart, and Epstein 2008). Through this adult-guided and student-focused process, children begin to see themselves as accomplished thinkers, decision makers, and problem solvers.

Utilizing an active learning approach in the TK classroom does not mean implementing a *laissez-faire* ("let them be") style of teaching (Miller and Almon 2009). Rather, student-initiated work balanced with thoughtful direct instruction maximizes learning. Children learn through relationships with supportive, skilled adults (Epstein 2007). The TK teacher observes, plans, and implements on-the-spot teaching based on work that is initiated by the student. In the opening vignette of this section, the teacher capitalized on a student's plan to craft a birthday gift for her mother by extending the project to include a writing task. Everyday play is rich in such academic learning, and with scaffolding it can be rich in language, literacy, mathematics, and problem solving if teachers carefully plan and facilitate experiences. A teacher first works from the student's interest to ensure a meaningful learning experience and builds upon this interest to extend opportunities for learning. Teachers who see themselves as facilitators of learning recognize the value of student's purposeful play, and they continually promote conceptual development through thoughtful support and scaffolding.

Summary

To meet students where they are and build on and extend what they know, it is imperative that TK teachers understand important milestones in child development as well as the overlapping nature of developmental domains. Teachers who are knowledgeable about the progression of cognitive, physical, social, emotional, and linguistic development are better able to plan learning experiences that engage TK students in meaningful discovery through play-based instruction. As demonstrated in UDL, engagement is the cornerstone of ensuring student access to the learning setting, and play is one approach for building student interest. Additionally, an awareness of motivation in early learning, with an emphasis toward creating a learning goal orientation, is central to fostering enthusiasm

for school and persistence in the face of difficulty. Educators who make it a priority to provide students with a wide variety of both student-initiated and teacher-guided learning opportunities meet young students' developmental needs and provide a strong foundation for their educational journeys. In this way, measurement of student outcomes can be monitored in an ongoing fashion throughout the day when incidental teaching opportunities emerge. Furthermore, how students demonstrate those critical milestones can be captured in the context of activities in which they are engaged.

Daily Routines

Young students thrive in settings that are predictable and consistent. In all TK classrooms, the daily routine and the schedule of events have an important influence on student behavior. A student's ability to engage, focus, and successfully complete tasks is especially contingent on routines and transitions that are consistent and balanced. Although consistent routines are important, flexibility may be necessary for students who need additional time to complete tasks. The TK year is one of growth and significant change in cognition and social–emotional competence. Sensitivity to the individual needs of students is important in shaping a routine that evolves to meet the developmental needs of children. Attention should be placed on varying the format of instruction, individual and group experiences, and organizing transitions (Thompson and Twibell 2009).

Structuring the Daily Routine

In comparison to older kindergarten students, most TK students have limited attention spans. They are in the early process of developing the impulse control required to focus on tasks that are not of their choosing. It is for this reason that TK teachers may consider beginning the year with more time dedicated to student-initiated work

Vignette

The students in Mr. Dao's TK classroom are preparing for a field trip to the local neighborhood market. During the class meeting, Mr. Dao reviews the visual schedule of the daily routine. "Today is a special day. As we talked about yesterday, we will be visiting the neighborhood market to help us plan our market in the Dramatic Play Area. I want to review our day with you one more time before we begin small-group work. First, we are having our class meeting (points to picture on schedule). Second, we will go to small groups (points to picture on schedule). Third, we will have choice time (points to picture on schedule). Fourth, instead of going outside (removes picture from schedule), we will go on our field trip (adds new picture of students walking together) to the neighborhood market." Mr. Dao repeats the field trip rules before dismissing them to small group. As a final cue, he adds, "I will post our daily routine back on the door if you need a visual reminder of our plan for the day."

and choice. Even as the year moves on, offering students multiple opportunities for purposeful play will continue to be an important part of the daily routine. A minimum of 45 minutes of uninterrupted choice time is considered best practice (Tomalison 2009). Student-initiated work should be balanced with teacher-directed learning experiences that are shorter in length and infused with integrated learning and movement. As students settle into the program structure, TK teachers can increase the length of adult instruction, while extending these learning concepts through hands-on, small-group experience. Furthermore, teachers should consider placing activities that require student focus and attention at the beginning of the day when students are fresh, alert, and ready to learn.

Facilitating Student Understanding of Routines and Transitions

While daily routines are important, the transitions that guide TK students from one activity or setting to another also warrant thoughtful consideration. As in all classrooms, the effective use of time is critical. When TK students are responsive to cues from adults and are able to engage in daily routines independently and transition smoothly, more time is available for learning and exploration. Therefore, to maximize student learning and engagement, teachers should carefully plan the length of time for learning activities and the number of transitions. Expectations for each routine and transition need to be thoughtfully planned and then taught, modeled, practiced, and reviewed as necessary. Instruction should be clear and concise and make use of auditory and visual cues to reinforce verbal prompts.

It is important for TK teachers to promote group and individual understanding of routines. For example, a visual schedule of the daily routine, one that includes photos of the routine and captions, could be posted at the eye level of students. Portable pictures (e.g., small, labeled photos on a binder ring) may also be distributed to students who require individual reminders of program activities. This format allows time for comprehension, and it offers individual support where necessary (e.g., "Tobin, let's look at our picture schedule. First we do small group, and then it's time to play outside").

Some students may struggle with managing their impulses and self-regulating their behavior to meet the classroom rules, especially during transitions. Implementing a short stretching and relaxation routine can assist students as they work to slow down their bodies and focus their attention. At the beginning of the school year, TK teachers may spend a great deal of time instructing students about acceptable behaviors during transitions (e.g., arrival, departure, cleanup, wait time, and in self-care routines). Songs, chants, and rhymes are useful strategies for teaching, cueing, and facilitating transitions. For example, the "cleanup song" indicates a change in routine and reminds all the students of their responsibilities during this time. Transitioning from an active experience to a quiet, more focused task may require additional teacher support as well. When a child exhibits difficulty in self-regulating, consider whether he or she needs additional support or modifications during transitions.

Students are also better able to meet standards for behavior when teachers prepare them for transitions (e.g., "Five more minutes until it will be time to clean up and move to your next activity"). Flexibility may be necessary when a student is fully engaged in an activity. A student who has been working with intense focus on an activity may need an additional minute to wrap-up the project before moving with the group. A brief check-in with the student can clarify the teacher's expectation for transition (e.g., "I see you need another minute. Please join us at large group as soon as you put your work at the 'work in progress' station").

Group Learning Experiences

Another important consideration in planning routines and transitions is accommodating the variations in group size that result from a thoughtfully responsive and engaging program. The size of the group should be contingent on the type of content being covered (Wasik 2008). Some learning experiences are better suited for individual exploration, while others are more

successfully implemented in small or large groups. During free choice time, students can choose to work independently or join others in cooperative projects. Those who are self-starters are able to move comfortably throughout the classroom, engaging in experiences that match their interest and temperament. TK teachers are then able to move in and out of interest areas, using these moments to extend the learning by engaging students in one-on-one conversation, problem solving, and inquiry (Jacobs and Crowley 2010).

Large-group experiences are ideally suited for promoting a sense of community, supporting conceptual development, and facilitating peer interactions. Whole-class instruction should focus on general introductions to concepts. The length of time for whole-classroom instruction should remain flexible and responsive to students' needs. For example, a teacher may elect to read a short book to the entire class to introduce the concept of patterns to students. The teacher could then follow up with a small-group activity that prompts students to revisit and practice the content that was introduced in the book. Group selection may vary over time. Heterogeneous groupings are an excellent opportunity for students to model for and mentor peers who may benefit from additional support. Homogeneous groupings allow teachers to target teaching strategies to specific learning needs. TK teachers need to plan flexible group formations throughout the routine to expose students to a wide range of experiences with their peers.

Summary

The structure and organization of the daily routine have a significant impact on student behavior and learning. TK teachers who plan for a balance of active and quiet experiences, alter the length of child-initiated and adult-directed learning to match developmental needs, and offer group instruction in different sizes and composition ensure an optimal learning experience for all students. Transitions, though brief by design, also require thoughtful preparation. The use of visual and auditory cues is an effective strategy for prompting students to follow the routine, and it supports the development of self-regulation skills.

An Overview of Selected Transitional Kindergarten Instructional Strategies

It is critical for educators to thoughtfully and intentionally select instructional strategies and activities that facilitate the delivery of TK curriculum content (see chapter 3). Effective instructional strategies (a) promote access to the content, (b) ensure active engagement with the materials and/or the teacher and peers, and (c) facilitate progress toward TK goals. This section provides an overview of selected instructional strategies that are applicable to most curricular areas and form a strong foundation for an effective TK program. The following strategies are discussed in this section:

1. Develop and reinforce oral language.

2. Scaffold tasks and skills appropriately, and then remove appropriate scaffolding gradually to challenge students beyond their current level of mastery.

3. Use think-alouds to model thoughtful reflection and to complement and balance free exploration and independent problem solving.

Cross-Curricular Instructional Strategies

Effective teachers draw upon a large repertoire of instructional strategies when they plan instruction. One of the major challenges for teachers is deciding which instructional strategies are most closely aligned with the identified academic and social–emotional needs and goals of their TK children. The strategies below were selected for inclusion in this guide because they are applicable across most subject areas and support the growth and development of all children (with appropriate modification). Although these strategies are appropriate for all TK students,

additional strategies for English learners will be discussed later in this chapter.

Strategies:

1. Develop and reinforce oral language development in all content areas. The role of oral language development in both children's emotional development and cognition is significant (Copple and Bredekamp 2009). When children have the oral language skills to both listen to and understand others and to respond appropriately to make their needs known, they are less like to experience frustration and more able to demonstrate self-regulation. As children's ability to orally comprehend and express language matures, they learn new vocabulary and gain more control over grammar and syntax (Epstein 2007). To support social–emotional, cognitive, and oral language development, teachers may take the following actions:

   • Intentionally introduce new words children might not encounter in everyday conversations and provide children with more accessible synonyms and examples of how the words are used (Copple and Bredekamp 2009).

   • Engage "individual children and groups in real conversation about their experiences, projects, and current events" (Copple and Bredekamp 2009, 157). One of the most effective strategies for engaging students in conversations is to invite interaction through thoughtful questions or comments. If students do not initiate conversation, the information in the following resource box may assist in promoting conversation.

   • Use "information" talk to narrate and describe what children are doing supports concept development and skill acquisition (Epstein 2007). For example, a teacher might say, "Jorge, I see that you are making a pattern with your blocks. You have a red, then a green, next a yellow, and finally a blue block. Then you repeat the pattern . . . red, green, yellow, and blue. Perhaps you and Sam can take turns making and copying patterns."

2. Scaffold tasks and skills appropriately to provide temporary support, then gradually decrease the scaffolding as children gain confidence and independence in completing the task.

> Excellent teachers use scaffolding to help children progress in all areas of learning and development throughout the day. And their scaffolding can take many forms. They might ask a question, point out a discrepancy, give a hint about an aspect of the problem or task that the child has missed, add a cue or support such as a picture or diagram, take a child's hand, or pair the child with a peer so that the two can be successful with their combined strength. (Copple and Bredekamp 2009, 39)

Children develop and learn most effectively when teachers intentionally focus instruction on the concepts and skills that lie just beyond their current independent level, "Development and learning advance when children are challenged to achieve at a level

A Suggested Model for Introducing Vocabulary

To bridge preschool foundations and kindergarten standards in science, Mr. Jeffers has been providing his TK students with opportunities to observe the physical properties of many objects and materials. He has decided to guide his students through an activity in which they will predict whether objects and materials will float or sink. Before he begins the demonstration, Mr. Jeffers needs to teach his students the meaning of the words *predict* and *prediction*.

He introduces the lesson by saying, "Yesterday, we talked about sinking and floating. Let's review what it means if something sinks. Remember, we have signals for sink and float. Show me what happens when something sinks (e.g., closed fist dropping rapidly into lap). Now show me what happens when something floats (e.g., flat hand gently rocking back and forth). We observed that a rock would sink in water and a piece of foil would float. Today we are going to predict whether other objects will sink or float in this glass bowl of water. To "predict" means to think about whether something will happen or not. When we predict whether something will happen or not, we make predictions. Let's say the words 'predict' and 'prediction.' Now let's say this sentence: 'When we predict that something will happen, we make predictions.' The important thing about predictions is that we think about something that might happen in the future."

Since he taught the concepts of "float" and "sink" following a similar instructional sequence the previous day, he quickly reviews their meaning. His students are now ready to examine a variety of objects and material, observe whether they float or sink, and create a class chart to record their predictions and the results of their experiment. To conclude the experience, Mr. Jeffers guides an engaging discussion to review and reinforce the meanings of the target words and to summarize their results. Mr. Jeffers knows that he will need to review these words frequently and encourage students to use them in future conversations with him and with their peers. He will also provide specific instruction in identifying support for predictions.

Using Questions to Promote Conversation

Use questions or verbal prompts thoughtfully and intentionally. If the goal is to check for understanding or elicit formative assessment evidence about gaps in their knowledge or conceptual understanding, consider questions or prompts that are narrowly targeted and aligned with your goal, for example:

- Tell me how many red blocks you have.

- Can you make a pattern like mine?

- Show me how you can jump on one foot.

- What is the first sound you hear in ____?

- Tell me what happened first in the story.

If, as described above, the goal is to promote extended conversations to expand and deepen children's thinking, encourage reflection, and invite further exploration and discovery, consider using open-ended questions such as these:

- What would happen if ____?

- What do you notice about ____?

- What do you know about ____?

- If you moved/changed/removed ____, what could happen?

- What is another way you could ____?

- Can you think of an example of ____?

- Tell me about what you have drawn/ made/constructed.

- What have you tried?

- What happened when you ____?

- What do you think about ____?

just beyond their current mastery, and also when they have many opportunities to practice newly acquired skills" (Copple and Bredekamp 2009, 15).

3. Use think-alouds to model alternative responses and strategies for dealing with challenges. Balance free exploration and independent problem solving with the use of intentionally planned think-alouds. When teachers think aloud, they verbalize their internal thoughts for children. Teachers slow the pace, pause to reflect, and orally model how he or she would think through a book, a difficult situation, or a challenging problem. The ultimate goal of think-alouds is to encourage students to internalize their own approaches to problem solving and to develop their own self-talk (Copple and Bredekamp 2009); however, many children initially need effective models. Consider applying a think-aloud approach across a wide variety of situations during the TK day. For example:

- As a teacher reads to the students and encounters a sentence with challenging syntax or difficult vocabulary, he or she might say, "I'm going to reread that sentence to make sure I understand what the author is telling me . . . Oh, now I understand. The author wants me to understand that ____."

- As a teacher discusses students' misunderstandings or social challenges, he or she might say, "I noticed that two of our friends wanted the same toy earlier today. Let me think. What would I have done if I were in that situation? I think I might have said, 'Sure, I'll share in a minute. Let's take turns' or 'Let's play with it together.' Or maybe I would have said, 'Let's stop and talk to the teacher about it.'"

- During phonemic awareness word play, a teacher might say, "Let me say that word

Provide Feedback to Support Self-Efficacy, Reflection, and Persistence

Providing students with detailed feedback, descriptive of actions and effort, helps them attend to and invest in their work and promotes self-assessment and self-efficacy (Gartrell 2007)—for example, "When you counted the collection you said there were 16 dinosaurs." Furthermore, educators can guide TK students to persist in tasks by providing encouragement and coaching (e.g., "Phew! That is a lot of dinosaurs. Let's count again together"). Offering students detailed reassurance gives insight to the process of learning (e.g., "Together we counted 15 dinosaurs. We had a different number the first time. Hmmm . . . Let's count one more time. Mathematicians often count their work twice"). As students accomplish goals, language and reinforcement should continue to focus on the students and their experiences. Instead of saying "Good job" to students, share observations with them and ask them questions. This invites students to elaborate and participate in their own reflective process. For example: "Fifteen! You got it! This time when you counted each dinosaur, you counted them once. What worked? . . . Yes, it looks like it helped to separate each dinosaur into a different pile after you counted them." This intentional use of teacher talk supports focused attention, encourages perseverance, and reflects a strong belief that, with highly skilled intentional guidance, all children are capable of learning. Persistence, effort, the use of program resources, and adult support all impact an individual's success (Galinsky 2010).

again slowly, so I can hear the very first sound. I think I will say it again. OK, I think I have it. Do you?"

- As a teacher models how to solve math problems, he or she might say, "Let me think. I have three blocks here on the table in front of me. José, will you put two more blocks on the table. Now, I want to know how many there are all together. So I will touch each one and say a number as I touch it. I think I will go slowly so I can be sure that I count correctly . . . Now, let me think again, the last number I said as I touched the last block was five, so I think there must be five blocks. I think I will count them one more time to make sure I am correct."

Summary

With thoughtful attention to the oral language environment, the appropriate use of scaffolding, and the balanced use of think-alouds, TK teachers support children's learning across curricular areas. A modified kindergarten curriculum that challenges students, provides an active and engaging learning environment, and utilizes effective instructional strategies will support TK students for success in kindergarten.

Transitional Kindergarten/ Kindergarten Combination Classrooms

TK/K combination classrooms are becoming a widespread reality as school district administrators work to expand the availability of TK programs at various school sites. In a classroom that includes both TK and traditional kindergarten students, differentiated instruction will be important for addressing the developmental diversity between the two groups of students. TK curriculum needs to focus on exposing students to California's Common Core State Standards for kindergarten, as well as the Content Standards for California Public Schools (kindergarten), while mastery of the standards is the focus for the kindergarten year. The needs of TK/K students will vary throughout the duration of the school year with diversity in skill and ability across both cohorts; teacher observations and professional collaboration are necessary to plan appropriately. This section will discuss strategies for creating collaborative workspaces and routines, differentiating instruction, and addressing family expectations. As teachers design an appropriate environment and plan responsive instruction for a TK/K combination class, they need to consider their class composition.

Environments and Routines in Transitional Kindergarten/Kindergarten Combination Classrooms

Initially, preparing for a TK/K combination classroom may seem challenging, but teachers can be reassured that many of the components used in TK classrooms benefit traditional kindergarten-age children. A place for gathering as a community, spaces designated for work in progress, displays of student work, and learning areas stocked with materials that comfortably challenge students are considered developmentally appropriate practice for early elementary classrooms (Copple and Bredekamp 2009). Such spaces, by design, permit flexibility and may be adapted over time to meet the differentiated instructional needs of all students. See chapter 6 for additional suggestions for differentiating instruction. For example, a Dramatic Play Area supplied with open-ended materials (e.g., cash register), and guided math and literacy experiences (e.g., coin sorting tray and word wall) invites a language-rich foundation as well as a focus on sorting, counting, and writing. How teachers structure and organize table activities can also encourage different entry points for learning. During small-group time, teachers can organize materials and differentiate activities designed for exposure and mastery.

Vignette

The students in Mrs. Peterson's TK/K classroom are busy at work. Activities are dispersed throughout the room. Some students assigned to work in small groups are practicing simple addition and subtraction skills. The small groups are made up of a mix of kindergarten and TK students. They assist one another in their work with some support from Mrs. Peterson, who moves about checking on individual and group progress. Elsewhere in the classroom, the remaining students work in different learning areas. Some students choose to play in the sensory bin counting the scoops of water needed to fill different containers. "This one didn't take as many scoops! Only five!" exclaims one child. At a different area, four students play a board game with a parent volunteer's assistance. Mrs. Peterson has strategically placed this adult to draw attention to math skills such as one-to-one correspondence and cardinality. "Let's count the number of dots on the dice together. One, two, three (they count on the first die) . . . four, five, six, seven, eight (adding the dots from the second die). You get to move eight spaces!" Two other groups of students play with Unifix Cube trays at the Math and Manipulatives Area and write numerals on the whiteboards at the Language and Literacy Area. In 20 minutes, Mrs. Peterson will transition the students to a large-group learning activity focused on letter and word recognition. She has carefully planned a lesson that will engage all learners—the TK students and the kindergarten students—at every stage of development and understanding.

Differentiated Learning Experiences for the Transitional Kindergarten/Kindergarten Classroom

The following activities are intended to illustrate methods for differentiating learning across the TK/K continuum. The same instructional materials and activities can be used to provide exposure to basic skills and concepts, as well as learning opportunities that are appropriate for students who are moving toward mastery. See chapter 6 for additional information related to differentiating instruction.

- Tangram blocks (California Preschool Learning Foundations, Geometry 1.2; Kindergarten Common Core, Geometry 5 and 6):

  » Exposure: Guide students to copy directly on top of a tangram design card.

  » Building toward mastery: Instruct students to first copy a design card on the desk top, and then find different ways to make the same design (i.e. use trapezoids instead of hexagons).

- Pattern stamps (California Preschool Learning Foundations, Algebra and Functions 2.1 and 2.2; also tied to Common Core Mathematical Practices):

  » Exposure: Guide students to use stamps to create an AB pattern.

  » Building toward mastery: Instruct students to use stamps to make more complicated patterns. Encourage students to write what type of pattern they have created.

- Journal writing (California Preschool Learning Foundations, Writing Strategy 1.1; Kindergarten Common Core, Standard Writing Strategies 1.1):

  » Exposure: Guide students to draw pictures to match the journal topic. Provide adult assistance to label student dictation.

  » Building toward mastery: Instruct students to draw and label their own words. Provide resources to support independent writing (e.g., word cards, picture dictionary).

Daily Routines and Grouping in Transitional Kindergarten/Kindergarten Combination Classrooms

The structure of the daily routine in the TK/K classroom should be adaptable to match learning needs. Initially, teachers may choose to create homogeneous groupings (e.g., small groups) based on grade level. It is likely, however, that even across ages and developmental stages in a TK/K classroom, students will possess different skill sets and abilities. Educators can modify these groups by mixing class cohorts based on the level of readiness demonstrated by individual students and opportunities for peer support (CDE 1999). There are many benefits to such multi-age groupings. Students in multi-age groups demonstrate greater patience and acceptance for variations in behavior and performance (Katz 1995). Furthermore, research suggests that "cognitive conflict arises when interacting children are at different levels of understanding" thus prompting a language-rich dialogue that will deepen knowledge and understanding for both students (Katz 1995). Teachers can coach skilled partners to scaffold learning for their peers by asking questions, providing feedback, and offering instruction (Gnadinger 2008). Where there is misinformation provided by a peer, teachers may step in to offer additional support and corrective feedback.

To promote a sense of friendship and community learning, teachers may want to include both cohorts in large-group instruction. Sensitivity to group needs will be needed as developmental readiness may dictate shorter segments of direct teaching to maintain the attention of the TK student. Most students respond positively to integrated lessons about letters, numbers, shapes, and other concepts embedded into music and movement learning experiences. Both TK and K students can be included in such dynamic instruction. Transitions, however, may prove particularly challenging for TK/K combination classrooms. Traditional kindergarten-age students tend to adapt quickly to classroom rules and routines, but some TK students may require more formal support and practice. Direct instruction and peer modeling will likely benefit the TK students as they settle into the classroom routine.

Foundational to program design and decision making in a TK/K classroom are teacher observation and professional collaboration (Lester 2005). To effectively meet all learners where they are, teachers should consider the chronological age of each student, with a focus on the individual stage of development across the continuum of learning. Teachers who observe, collect a variety of student work samples, and use developmentally appropriate standardized assessment tools are able to adjust the rigor of the curriculum to match individual and group needs. They challenge all learners to accomplish tasks at a level that is just beyond their current mastery and offer students opportunities for repetition to become proficient at recently acquired skills (Copple and Bredekamp 2009, 15). Furthermore, teachers who coordinate efforts with school staff avoid redundant curriculum in the traditional kindergarten year for TK students. For example, a teacher familiar with specific traditional kindergarten seasonal activities (e.g., Five Little Pumpkins), may choose to modify the curriculum to a different area of focus (e.g., Five Little Apples) while still emphasizing the same standards for learning.

Communicating Expectations for Transitional Kindergarten/Kindergarten Combination Classes

TK programs are new to most families. Designed with the intent to provide a two-year learning experience, parents of students enrolled in TK/K programs may express confusion about the design, purpose, and formation of the combination classroom. Additionally, TK parents may not understand guidelines for kindergarten promotion, assuming their child will move from TK directly to first grade. To establish and maintain positive home–school partnerships, teachers must communicate openly and frequently with families. A TK/K parent orientation can explain the educational and curricular progression, the benefits of mixed-age groupings, and long-term goals for students' education. Providing a two-year kindergarten program takes into account individual needs and promotes exposure and mastery opportunities for every student. Administrators and teachers can encourage families to become involved in their children's education through volunteer opportunities at home and school. The more families are engaged in school events and the more informed they are about classroom curriculum, the more likely they are to understand and appreciate the value of the TK year and the benefits of participating in a combination classroom.

Summary

TK/K combination classrooms present unique challenges but offer many positive opportunities for learning. Students, families, and professionals have much to gain from participating in mixed-age programs. There are many potential benefits as former TK students move into a combined TK/K or traditional kindergarten classroom. With a greater understanding of classroom routines, former TK students may exhibit more confidence as they approach new learning experiences and serve as leaders and role models to their peers. To meet the different learning needs of students, teachers who are assigned to TK/K classrooms should create environments, routines, and curriculum that are structured but also flexible. Observation will play an integral role in designing appropriate activities and experiences to match emergent learning needs. Parents have an important role to play and contribute to the success of a combination classroom. Their understanding of program design and their active investment can do much to encourage students and teaching staff.

Students with Disabilities

All TK students are considered as valued members of their classroom community. Students with disabilities are at greater risk for exclusion by their peers and often require more intensive support than some teachers may initially be equipped to offer (Guralnick 1999; Odom 2000; Odom, Buysse, and Soukakou 2011). Participating in IEP meetings, building close partnerships with families, seeking resources from specialists, and engaging in regular, reflective practice will build professional competencies in serving students with disabilities. Furthermore, teachers who understand that all students benefit from differentiated instruction will find that the tools, curriculum, and routines they use to support typically developing children are easily adapted or modified to accommodate students with disabilities. Strategies for inclusive practices are described and resources to better support all diverse learners are offered in this section.

Inclusive Practices

Inclusion is a classroom model and a philosophical approach that embraces the notion that all children, regardless of differences, belong in classrooms with their same age peers. Inclusive practices are techniques that ensure successful integration of each student into the classroom culture and provide access to core curriculum. For all students to have a beneficial and rewarding educational experience, teachers need to make

Vignette

After attending the IEP meeting for Jack, Mr. Arimoto takes a moment to reflect on what he has learned about Jack's strengths, areas in need of support, and his family's goals for the upcoming academic year. Mr. Arimoto has worked with students with similar sensory needs before, but he wants to make sure his efforts are tailored to Jack's personal style. From what his preschool teacher shared, Jack responds well to visual cues and occasionally needs sensory breaks to regulate his behavior and attention. Mr. Arimoto makes a mental note to create several small picture schedules and to gather a collection of squeeze balls for Jack as well as for other students. He begins to craft a plan to introduce squeeze balls to the students so that they understand their use in the classroom and so they can choose to use them as needed. Mr. Arimoto also writes down a list of questions to ask the district occupational therapist and resource specialist about additional ideas for program support.

sure that the environment, instructional practices, materials, and routines are appropriately matched to individual and group needs. Beginning with a UDL model, TK teachers consider a variety of ways to present information so that all learners are engaged in and attentive to the subject matter. Examples of representation include graphic images of concepts and information, real pictures attached to words, three-dimensional object displays of lessons, and large-group demonstration followed by small-group work on the concept. Different methods of instruction may be used to spark and sustain interest in the learning activity. For instance, exposure to letters may take the form of puppetry, a song, picture book, movement activities, sandpaper letters, picture cards, and small-group instruction. Furthermore, TK teachers measure performance by providing multiple avenues for the student to demonstrate progress. Students with disabilities may need assistive technology devices (such as an electronic tablet app) to demonstrate understanding of an academic concept. For example, students may use an electronic tablet app to identify the letter of the day among other letters or use a computer game with a touch screen to select letter options. Once the TK teacher has implemented a UDL strategic plan for the classroom environment and instructional techniques for all children, individual adaptations may then be considered based on the needs of individual students as demonstrated in the vignette.

After the classroom and teaching instruction has been modified according to a UDL framework, TK teachers may explore additional changes to the environment and the method of instruction that need to take place for individual children with special needs. For example, learning areas and individual cubbies that are labeled with pictures of activities and materials promote access for all children by providing visual cues. A student with autism, for instance, may need a "first/then" visual schedule to help with transitions from one activity to the next. A picture of the current activity is presented along with the preferred activity that will follow, offering a sequence of events from one learning area to the next. The process of creating an inclusive classroom begins with incorporating items such as photos, literature, and play props that reflect children's different abilities (Derman-Sparks and Edwards 2010). Just as representing all cultures and linguistic backgrounds in program design influences a student's sense of self, so too does integrating the real experiences of people with special needs. These inclusive images match an anti-bias curriculum approach and should be in place in all programs, regardless of whether students with disabilities are enrolled in the class.

In a TK classroom, students with special needs may require adjustments to the teaching instruction

and the classroom setting for greater access, participation, and belonging to occur. The physical layout and selection of materials may need to be modified to invite all learners into the discovery process. For instance, students who use adaptive equipment for development of gross-motor skills need ample space to enter into learning areas and freedom of movement throughout the classroom. To support students with sensory and/or behavioral management needs, educators should also assess the amount of visual and auditory stimulation (Bakley 2001). Cluttered visual fields, excessively noisy play, and crowded furnishings can contribute to off-task behavior and poor quality of work. Adaptive writing tools, play equipment, and manipulatives can be made readily available to allow students to work from a place of comfort and competence. A toolbox of materials may help TK teachers to make quick adjustments to the environment or materials. The following basic items are recommended for the toolbox (Sadao and Robinson 2010):

- 3-inch binders
- Small (½-inch), self-sticking fabric dots and strips
- Battery interrupter for battery-operated toys
- Binder clips for page turners
- Double-sided carpet tape
- Furniture bumpers for page fluffers
- Highlighter tape

- Hot-glue gun with glue sticks
- Laminating paper
- Microfiber mitt
- Nonglare page savers
- Nonslip shelf liner
- Simple and adaptive switches for devices
- Small photograph album
- Sponge rollers
- Sticky-back foam
- Voice-recording modules

TK teachers may also consider downloading a free guide, *Adaptations in Action: Adaptation Bin for Children* (Nielsen 2009), to support students with disabilities in the classroom.

Inclusive routines are flexible and utilize multi-sensory strategies for learning and behavior management. Visual cues, such as picture schedules or hand signs, may be used by teachers to remind students of program expectations and to offer choices for engagement. For example, a symbol card with a listening ear and another one with a red stoplight can be used to cue students when it is time to listen and when a behavior is undesirable during a large-group activity. Auditory prompts (e.g., transition music or chimes) also help students focus and meet the expectations of classroom rules. Educators who assign peer partners for collaborative work/play encourage the development of friendship skills for all students. Motivational strategies such as "good choice" charts reinforce self-regulation skills and highlight developmental progress over time. Additional methods for

supporting a student's individual needs can be created in collaboration with families, school specialists, and community resource partners. Additional ideas for assistive technology strategies focused on play and learning, communication, and literacy can be found in Sadao and Robinson (2010).

Resources and Collaborative Partnerships

Communication and collaboration are essential for ensuring that students with disabilities receive appropriate and high-quality education. In addition to establishing important relationships with families and stakeholders, IEP meetings inform teachers of current student needs, goals for learning, suggested practices for inclusion, and curriculum modifications. Depending on the type of disability, a follow-up conversation with the school's resource specialist may offer additional ideas for accommodating a student's individual needs. Ongoing open communication among all involved parties is essential to tracking development, updating goals, and planning for the next steps. Regular meetings between the TK teacher, special education teacher, and other specialists allow teaching teams to share effective

strategies both in and out of the classroom setting. Informal conversation, e-mail, phone calls, and an interactive journal are just a few of the many ways teachers can maintain two-way communication with families. Administrators must also stay informed of the progress of students with disabilities. The continual support of administrators for general and special education staff promotes collaboration among staff serving students with disabilities.

Summary

Creating inclusive TK classrooms means that teachers thoughtfully prepare an environment that reflects students of all abilities and permits access to curriculum in a way that is both appropriate and functional for all. Flexible routines, intentional prompts and cues, and collaborative work encourage all learners as they seek to be active participants in the classroom setting. At the root of inclusive work is communication and collaboration with families, specialists, school administrators, and other community stakeholders.

Students Who Are English Learners

California has a diverse population of young learners from varied linguistic and cultural backgrounds. Teachers of TK students recognize the value of diversity and show respect for each child's home culture and language by incorporating familiar words, objects, and images into program and curricular design. At the same time, they continually encourage the development of English language and literacy skills. Creating family and community partnerships for children who are learning English is also an important goal for educators. Teachers make use of dynamic instructional strategies that engage different modalities to bridge linguistic backgrounds. They provide concrete tools for making sense of and acquiring skills in the English language. Strategies for encouraging home–school connections, as well as inclusive practices for English learners, are discussed in this section.

Vignette

Ms. Wilson gathers her TK students for shared-book reading time. She positions herself at the front of the group, slightly raised in her chair so that all students have access to the illustrations in the big book and her visual props. Approximately half of the students in the class speak a language other than English at home. Before Ms. Wilson begins reading, she brings out puppets and real objects to introduce new English vocabulary from the story. "Today we are going to read a story about a hermit crab (holding up a puppet of a hermit crab). Let's all say 'hermit crab,' okay?" After prompting the students' choral response, Ms. Wilson continues, "What do you see on our hermit crab?" A young boy says "pincher" in Spanish and then moves his fingers together in a claw-like movement. The teacher responds, "Yes, Vicente! The hermit crab has claws (pointing to the puppet's claw) that pinch. Let's all make our hands into claws (mimicking Vicente's movement). We are pinching our claws like a hermit crab." Ms. Wilson introduces a few more words with props: She introduces 'shell' by using a real hermit-crab shell, and she introduces 'ocean' by showing pictures of the beach and underwater scenes. She then proceeds to read the story, using dynamic tones and gestures.

The Role of Families and Communities

A child's identity and sense of self is closely tied to his or her cultural and linguistic heritage. How children view themselves and their perception of how others view them can have a lasting influence on the value they place on their home culture. Research has highlighted the benefits of being fluent in two or more languages. Students who speak more than one language demonstrate advanced cognitive skills, sophisticated linguistic abilities, and show lasting ties to their family culture (CDE 2007; Nemeth 2012). TK teachers can communicate deep respect and appreciation for diversity by forming authentic partnerships with families and neighboring communities. Personal conversations are essential to the establishment of quality connections, but language barriers and/ or lack of understanding of cultural norms can work against this important goal. Educators utilize a variety of strategies to overcome these potential obstacles to collaboration.

Welcoming families with diverse backgrounds is important (Espinosa 2010). Calling family members by name and learning key words in each family's home language shows a commitment to families and respect for linguistic diversity. As parents feel comfortable, they can be invited to assist in the construction of the language and literacy environment. They can label material, take dictation, and read books or retell stories in the home language. Some families may elect to assist the TK classroom through more active, less language-focused tasks such as assisting with the preparation of classrooms materials or by sending donations for classroom use, such as recyclables or books in their home language. Educators strengthen home learning experiences by reinforcing the value of speaking, reading, writing, and simply playing together as a family in the home language.

Community volunteers can also support program efforts to enhance language learning. Children who have a strong foundation in their primary language

more easily learn to use a second language (CDE 2009b; Tabors and Snow 2001). Volunteers who speak the children's home language(s) can participate in classroom activities, using both English and the primary language to help English learners feel more at ease. While doing so, they promote shared understanding and expansion of vocabulary. It is also important for families to have access to program resources, including written documents and take-home learning experiences. To maximize family engagement, written communications should be translated into the family's home language.

Strategies to Support English Language Development

Although some of the vocabulary and oral language development strategies presented in this section are similar to those discussed earlier in this chapter, they are discussed here as well, with the addition of English learner examples to emphasize their importance. "Achieving academic success in school includes developing a knowledge and mastery of formal schooling practices in addition to building on one's home or community language practices. All children can have high levels of achievement if provided with a rich challenging curriculum and appropriate forms of assistance" (CDE 2007). Language is learned through conversation and by engaging in real contexts. "The child is an active party in the language-learning process . . . His experience and interaction with others give him the background to relate language to the sound/meaning relationship and to the purpose it represents" (Clark 2000, 181). Student-initiated, purposeful play is an informal framework for building English vocabulary. When teachers use running commentary as students work with manipulatives, label real objects, and elaborate on students' efforts to communicate in English or a home language, they help to support students' understanding of the structure of English. Affect, tone, and gestures offer additional information for processing new words and making sense of experiences—for example, when a teacher says, "Yes, that is an alligator. It is a very BIG alligator. I see it has sharp teeth, too [pointing to the alligator's teeth]!"

English learners may need extra assistance as they seek to participate in peer play. The presence of a teacher or another supportive adult can help students as they work across different languages. "Christopher is pointing to the truck. I think he would like it. Christopher, say, 'I like the truck. May I have a turn?'" Peers can also scaffold language development. Pairing English learners with a socially skilled peer provides them with a model for action (e.g., I see, I do). Visual aids may be used to assist students as they work to meet classroom rules and resolve social conflicts. A teacher observes the student holding the solution kit and responds, "Maya, what is your idea for solving this problem? Oh, you are showing us the picture of children playing together. You want to share the cash register."

Formal instruction, such as shared-book reading and large-group learning, also requires the use of clear, descriptive language. Students are better able to attend to shared-book reading when they are first introduced to important vocabulary using pictures or real objects. Time can be set aside in advance for teachers to pre-teach new words and pre-read book content. Inflection, pointing to illustrations, and dramatizing text are additional ways to engage English learners during the large-group reading experience. Visual cues remind students of expectations for action during teacher-initiated instruction. A picture of an ear indicates that it is time to listen, and a picture of a raised hand models how to ask for a turn to speak. Incorporating repetition and opportunities to practice helps all children build knowledge and fluency, but is especially effective with English learners. Rereading stories and singing familiar songs and chants will increase participation and enthusiasm for group learning experiences. TK teachers can further include students in the language learning process by prompting them to demonstrate understanding with gestures and movement (e.g., "Show me what 'cruising' looks like. Yes, we are moving our bodies slowly, just floating around").

Children become fluent in a second language at different rates. Motivation, personality, age, and exposure to practice influence the process (Tabors and Snow 2001). For example, students who are temperamentally "slow to warm" may take more time to express themselves in the new language than extroverted peers; however, slow progress should not be considered a delay in learning, but instead a reflection of the students' unique personalities. Effective educators use their observations of preferred learning style, interests, and readiness to inform their instruction. Allowing English learners wait time to process verbal and written prompts is important in creating a comfortable learning climate.

Summary

Supporting English learners involves communicating value and respect for the home language while simultaneously nurturing fluency in English. Establishing authentic partnerships with families and community volunteers adds depth to program curriculum and encourages the continued use and development of the student's primary language. Oral language is at the heart of instruction, using real contexts and objects to promote vocabulary development and increase shared meaning. Students learning a new language benefit from the use of visual tools and repetition in instruction. Teachers maximize student learning when they maintain an awareness of individual development and attend to individual cues for additional prompts and verbal coaching.

Teacher–Family–Community Engagement: A Key to Effective Transitional Kindergarten Instruction

The relationships that educators establish with students, their families, and their communities have a lasting impact on long-term development and educational success (Henderson and Mapp 2002). The relationships that are fostered in this introductory school experience will facilitate the comfort and trust of students and families in school systems and will communicate important messages about the value of family input and involvement in education (Pianta and Kraft-Sayre 2003). The specific relationship between strong parent and family engagement and highly effective TK instruction will be discussed in this section. Additional strategies for building warm, personal relationships with families and communities will be provided in chapter 7.

Nurturing Family Connections to Enrich Instruction

The comfort a family feels in an educational setting contributes to a student's sense of trust

Vignette

Mrs. Coady anxiously stands at her classroom window and awaits the arrival of her "summer play date" group. She has invited four students and their families to school to spend some time in the TK play yard prior to the start of the academic year. She intends to use this time to watch the students at play, attend to their interests in play and friendship skills, and engage the families in casual conversations about their home culture, family pastimes, and goals for education. The important information she gathers and meaningful relationships she creates with the students and families will help her prepare an effective curriculum and classroom environment for the upcoming school year.

and security. The teacher's knowledge of family relationships, the rich traditions they share, and the goals that parents and families hold for their child's future all need to be considered when teachers create the TK learning environment and align the curriculum with appropriate instructional strategies. Parents have valuable information about their child's personality, interests, and skills. Teachers who partner with families can use this information to better inform their work in the classroom (Bennett 2007).

Teachers can create genuine opportunities to learn this information from families. Informal conversations before the school year begins— during home visits, school play dates, or at a classroom open house—are ways to initiate home–school connections (Jacobs and Crowley 2010). A formal questionnaire may also be used to supplement information gained from these conversations. As teachers learn additional information about a child's skills and traits from parents and ask about their goals and expectations for the child, they gain valuable insights that can help to guide their teaching practice. This ongoing flow of information between parents and TK teachers facilitates a rich and responsive learning environment.

When teachers make decisions about the most appropriate instructional strategies to deliver TK curriculum and about the most effective experiences to prepare children for a traditional kindergarten program, information from parents should be taken into consideration. TK teachers continually refine and enhance the learning environment and build their repertoire of teaching strategies to ensure that their instruction is culturally relevant and builds a strong foundation for student success.

Building Community Connections to Enrich Instruction

Community connections can further teacher awareness of group values, strengths, and needs. A school's surrounding community also has a direct influence on the school, the student, and the family. Studies on community engagement show that when "communities mobilize around school improvement efforts many positive outcomes can be achieved, including improved student achievement" (Iowa School Boards Foundation 2007). In addition to local businesses' financial support of school programs, educators can take community involvement one step further by utilizing local talents, knowledge, and expertise to enhance school curriculum. Inviting guest speakers, planning field trips to neighboring areas of interest, and coordinating community projects, such as a cooperative garden, are just a few of the many ways to highlight the school as a community entity. TK teachers, particularly those who do not live in the community where they are employed, can attend local events to understand the context for child development, family life, and community needs and values. This information can be used in program design and curriculum planning.

Reflecting on Culturally Relevant Education

The learning environments that teachers create and the curriculum they implement have an important impact on student learning. In particular, research indicates differences between home experiences and school culture negatively influence minority children's academic achievement (York 2003). Teachers can design learning spaces and lesson plans with regard to individual learning style, family diversity, and community values. As TK teachers prepare their programs, the following questions warrant thoughtful consideration and deep reflection (York 2003):

- Does the classroom reflect students' daily lives?

- Do activities incorporate students' home language(s), culture, and community?

- Does the curriculum inspire students to learn about their family and home culture?

Summary

Highly effective TK teachers seek and continually engage families as partners in fostering the development of children. They value the information shared by parents and use it to strengthen their teaching. When TK teachers incorporate culturally responsive practices into their daily instruction and interactions with children, the program is enriched and student learning is enhanced.

CHAPTER 5
The Transitional Kindergarten Learning Environment

The Transitional Kindergarten Learning Environment
http://www4.scoe.net/ims/webcasts/cf/index.
cfm?fuseaction=archivedDetail&eventID=140&archiveID=254

The Transitional Kindergarten Learning Environment (YouTube with Captions)
http://www.youtube.com/watch?v=c_x80Z9Alps

The TK classroom environment sets the stage for learning and interactions between students and adults. It also establishes the expectations for behavior in the classroom (Thompson and Twibell 2009). An attractive, well-organized classroom invites students to actively explore and engage with the materials and access classroom instruction. Carefully selected, age-appropriate materials build the conceptual knowledge of TK students, and are directly related to skills and content in the California Preschool Learning Foundations, California's Common Core State Standards for kindergarten, and Content Standards for California Public Schools (kindergarten). TK teachers who purposefully incorporate elements of students' home cultures and diverse experiences into the classroom environment encourage and establish levels of comfort and security (Riley et al. 2008). Thoughtful consideration should be given to the needs of individual students such as accessible spaces and activities, multi-sensory materials, and

Vignette

After finishing whole-group English language arts instruction, it is choice time in Mr. Ting's classroom. Students are spread throughout the room engaging in a variety of activities in the different learning areas. A small group of students builds an elaborate tower with blocks in the Construction Area. Nearby, another group prepares "dinner" in the Dramatic Play Area using empty food containers that were donated by families. Across the room, two students work in parallel at the Writing Area. They occasionally turn to converse with one another about their individual letter writing. Mr. Ting scans the environment and then kneels down next to students who are sketching pictures of the silkworm habitat in the Science and Discovery Area. He comments on the different details highlighted in their drawings and encourages the students to use the magnifying lenses to closely examine the silkworm cocoons. He pauses as he watches to see how the students respond to his suggestion. He then moves over to engage with students in the Mathematics and Manipulatives Area where he is able to closely observe and coach two students playing a board game. At the same time, he also notices the skills utilized by another student playing a pre-reading game in the Computer Area.

regulating routines that ensure successful learning experiences for all students.

Incorporating student ideas, work, and experiences into the environment will support and bring about effective teaching and learning. Specific strategies are discussed in this chapter for planning indoor learning areas and outdoor spaces. Emphasis is placed on the selection and presentation of open and closed-ended learning materials and the display of students' important work.

The Transitional Kindergarten Classroom

As stated in the Transitional Kindergarten Planning Guide, the "TK year should include a modified kindergarten program based on evidence-based practices" (CCSESA 2011,19). The social–emotional development of the TK student must be kept in mind when learning environments are created. The classroom should include a balance of space for direct-instruction as well as opportunities for student-initiated exploration and active learning. The spaces designated for choice in the TK classroom must be more structured than what would be found in a preschool program, and they should include materials that highlight and introduce concepts from the California Preschool Learning Foundations, California's Common Core State Standards for kindergarten, and Content Standards for California Public Schools (kindergarten). This intentional approach to promote structured choice permits exposure to the standards while still facilitating active learning.

The TK classroom needs designated spaces for large-group instruction as well as areas for small-group learning and individual exploration (CDE 2011; Copple and Bredekamp 2009). A large rug in a central location makes an ideal spot for students to gather as a classroom community to sing songs, engage in movement experiences, and participate

in letter and number games. A small space with a bookshelf works well as a quiet nook for reading stories. Additional areas for learning can include spaces for writing, constructing with blocks, art, science, and manipulatives.

Several different terms are used to refer to these areas—for example, "centers," "learning areas," and "work stations." The particular term used to refer to these learning spaces is a program and teacher decision that relates to the language of the daily routine. For consistency and clarity in this document, these spaces are called *learning areas*. The specific learning areas referenced in this document are the Construction Area, Reading Area, Listening Area, Language and Literacy Area, Art Area, Computer Area, Science and Discovery Area, Math and Manipulatives Area, Sensory Area, and the Dramatic Play Area.

When teachers consider the different spaces in the classroom, universal design concepts are paramount for creating learning areas that are free of clutter and barriers. Using the three components of universal design for learning (UDL), the TK teacher is able to orchestrate an organized and manageable work environment where all children can move freely between learning areas and readily participate in activities. The first step is to think about how to engage the student in a task; this is done by constructing spaces that can be readily changed if a child with a wheelchair has difficulty reaching materials.

Questions to Guide the Arrangement of the Classroom to Support Access for All Children (Sadao and Robinson 2010)

Overall Environment

- Are there any large physical barriers that obstruct movement between learning areas?
- Are the pathways from the entrances to the learning areas and other seat locations wide enough?
- Does each table have room for adapted furniture, seats, and wheelchairs?
- Can a child with visual or motor issues navigate the classroom environment with minimal teacher assistance?
- Does each learning area have picture labels and directions to guide students about what to do in that area?
- Are storage containers labeled so that toys and games can be used and put away easily?

Student Cubbies

- Does each cubby have a student's picture and name on it?
- Do students have easy access to hooks for clothes and backpacks?
- Does each cubby have a small shelf or additional box to hold the student's work and journal?

Computer Stations

- Do computer stations accommodate students who need special seating?
- Are there additional cushions and other materials that could be used to adjust a child's seating position?
- Does the seating arrangement allow for more than one child at a computer station?
- Is there a touch screen that can be used in lieu of a mouse?
- When seating adjustments have been made for a student with motor issues, do all students still have access to the computer(s)?
- Are computer stations situated within view of a teacher?

Small-Group Thematic Areas

- Is there a tray or small plastic pool to provide a confined space for blocks?
- Do some blocks have self-sticking fabric strips for added balance during stacking and building activities?
- Is the art area stocked with a variety of adapted scissors, pencil and paintbrush grips, and colored tape?
- Does each table have laminated written rules and picture cues providing directions to students?

Group Lesson Area

- Is a schedule posted with picture cues?
- Are individual schedules posted for students who need further individualization?
- Are pointers and flashlights available for pointing out and highlighting important information presented during large-group activities?
- Is a rain stick or timer available for providing an auditory cue when transitions occur?
- Is there a defined space for large-group activities identified by a large carpet or carpet squares?
- Are there a variety of props and other instructional materials to actively engage students in large-group learning?

When a child is involved in an activity, the second step is to provide a variety of materials focused on a particular learning concept. For instance, in the story about Mr. Ting's learning areas, offering students several sizes of magnifying glasses that have sponge rollers attached to the grips allows for easier grabbing and maintaining hold on the object. Large pictures of silk worms and their habitat provide another way of representing the concept. The third consideration in UDL is providing each student with different ways of expressing their understanding of a topic.

For a child with limited language skills, creating a voice-activated communication device with four audio cued picture choices of the silk worm and other insects offers a way for the child to select the silk worm picture they observed to indicate recognition of the concept. Keeping room arrangement and the potential need for accommodating the learning environment in mind will avoid challenges with accessibility and potential behavioral outbursts later on. Guiding questions highlighted in this section provide a rubric for adapting the learning areas to accommodate all learners.

Principles of Design

Before moving furniture and arranging the materials, TK teachers can use several guiding principles to plan spaces. Educators should begin by closely reviewing the fixed features of the indoor space of the classroom. The locations of doors, sinks, built-in cabinets, and large whiteboards will often dictate the plans for organizing the space. The Art Area and Sensory Area should be placed as close as possible to the child-size sinks because of the messy nature of the activities that take place in those areas. Access to the large whiteboard is important for large-group learning experiences. Storage for students' personal items and family communication should be located near the classroom entrance. After the initial placement of learning areas based on fixed features, teachers can define spaces according to the type of play. Active

spaces (e.g., Construction Area, Dramatic Play Area) should be grouped together to promote more focused play in other locations of the classroom (Harms, Clifford, and Cryer 2005). Clearly defined and labeled areas communicate expectations for play, contain materials within the area, and create a traffic flow for movement between spaces. The placement of furniture, tables and shelving, as well as visual markers such as signs and carpeting further guide behavior. For example, a medium-size rug placed in front of a shelf of blocks not only offers a soft space to work on the floor, but it also suggests a reasonable work station and the blocks stay on the rug.

Group size is an important factor in the creation of distinct areas for learning (Thompson and Twibell 2009). Thoughtful consideration should be given to the number of students who can participate in a particular space for exploration. While these will be classroom/teacher specific decisions, generally the Language and Literacy Area may be smaller in size than the Dramatic Play Area. The Science and Discovery Area may be similar in size to the Math and Manipulatives Area. Tables used to support area activities as well as small-group learning experiences will also dictate area size. Once initial arrangements have been made, teacher observation will confirm the efficacy of the design or modifications may be needed. Visual systems that communicate appropriate group size to students are also beneficial for managing areas. Examples include picture boards with sticky fabric

Aesthetics in Quality Learning Environments

An often overlooked area of program planning is the aesthetics and organization of the learning environment. The physical layout facilitates exploration and supports classroom management. The choice of wall displays, furnishings, and organization of materials has an impact on students' learning and behavior (Bakley 2001; Curtis and Carter 2003). Creating a visually pleasing and inviting environment for students and adults is important. Additionally, the placement of familiar objects and images creates a sense of warmth and security for young children.

- Tools for assessing program quality generally examine the physical layout of the classroom and the location and quantity of materials; little attention is given to the organization, grouping, and display of items. The following basic guidelines can help facilitate the creation of a visually pleasing and educationally effective space:

- Choose neutral colors for tables, chairs, and other furnishings to create a natural palette from which to incorporate learning materials, and highlight important documents and student work (Hohmann and Weikart 2002).

- Limit the use of color. Too much color and overwhelming displays on walls make it difficult to focus; the eye is drawn to move across the space to the next stimulating exhibit rather than hone in on the informative display. A note of caution, particularly for the beginning of the school year: less is more.

- Design the classroom walls with carefully selected textures and postings. For example, a quilt or cultural artifact such as a woven rug hung in the Dramatic Play Area offers warmth and a feeling of home. A cork or magnet board in the Construction Area, with copies of blueprints and photos of inspiring real structures, as well as space for "current work" from the students, suggests potential projects and is flexible for changing images over time.

- Add living things (e.g., plants, flowers, and pets) to enliven the indoor environment.

TK teachers can assess their classroom environment by taking a simple inventory of their space and reflecting on the following questions:

- Are the aesthetics of the environment inviting? Do they welcome the students, families, and teachers?

- Are materials and visuals placed at the students' eye level?

- Is the environment calming, or would it tend to overstimulate students?

- Is the environment clean and well organized?

- Does the environment reflect the culture, traditions, history, and identity of the children, families, and teachers in the community?

TK educators may face limitations in terms of budget, classroom furnishings, and program materials, but each TK classroom should evolve over time to meet learning goals and emergent themes. The physical layout of the classroom can be modified to support changes in behavior and curriculum as needed. Both short- and long-term plans could be created for the aesthetic design, and TK teachers can solicit donations and integrate new items. Students, families, and educators will find new satisfaction in the space they have co-created; they will find that student learning and engagement justify the time spent on improving program aesthetics.

strips or name sticks with numbered openings so that students will know if there is space available in the learning area.

TK teachers also need to consider the importance of visual access. A clear visual field permits teachers to easily scan the learning environment and select individual students or groups that may benefit from additional support or instruction. Furthermore, educators can observe and assess students' development as children pursue student-initiated work or engage in structured, teacher-initiated learning experiences. Students will benefit from low shelving and limited visual barriers (Hohmann and Weikart 2002). They should be able to view peers at work and join activities that match their emerging interests and preferences for exploration. Classroom prompts (e.g., posted alphabet, behavioral charts) provide important tools for action or social support and should be easily viewed by and accessible to all students.

Materials

Supplying the TK classroom with a variety of rich and engaging materials promotes concrete learning and provides students with experiences that enable them to meet the expectations outlined in the California Preschool Learning Foundations, California's Common Core State Standards for kindergarten, and Content Standards for California Public Schools (kindergarten). Both open- and close-ended materials serve a purpose in TK students' learning (Thompson and Twibell 2009).

Close-ended materials, such as puzzles, activity boards, and matching games, promote conceptual development through guided learning experiences. Close-ended materials have a specific purpose and outcome; within the structure of the material there is inherently one right answer. Teachers can incorporate close-ended materials into choice time, and they can work these activities into the small-group rotations to promote independent learning. In addition to close-ended materials, students should have access to a large number of open-ended materials. These are materials that focus on the process of discovery and allow students to express their creativity (e.g., textiles, inch blocks, recyclables, and the like). If the room allows, educators could reserve a space for the "work in progress" of various students. This designated space protects students' work and offers opportunities to revisit and expand on these projects.

TK teachers set the stage for student learning by organizing and displaying materials into conceptual groups. Placing like materials next to each other provides students with important information about the purpose and possible use of the items (Riley et al. 2008). For example, in the Science and Discovery Area, placing the magnifying lenses on the shelf next to a basket of natural materials collected from the outdoor environment invites students to take a closer look. Additionally, teachers can intentionally group items to emphasize learning of specific content standards. In the Math and Manipulatives Area, creating an attractive display of flat tangram pieces and geometric solid shapes and then placing one item in a "mystery box" invites students to describe the defining characteristics of the hidden object and make comparisons with the other shapes on display.

Materials made available for students' independent use can be clearly labeled. Labels may be created in a variety of formats, but all could include some form of print and an image of the specific material (e.g., picture, clip art, or hand-drawn image). A picture of the material paired with the written word exposes students to environmental print (Ranweiler 2004), while also allowing students at all levels of reading ability to select materials for use. Labeling materials also supports student participation in caring for the classroom environment as they are able to cleanup activities and return them to the designated space when finished. Furthermore, labeling creates a universally designed classroom that is easily accessible by all learners. To ensure the materials are designed with all learners in

mind, refer to "Ideas for Supporting Additional Accommodations for Learning" on the next page.

As mentioned previously, TK teachers can create learning areas throughout the classroom that invite students to explore and engage with the content standards. Where possible, these learning areas can be supplied with real objects that represent the diverse backgrounds and cultures of the classroom family community (e.g., visual art, fabrics, food containers). Meaningful materials

"Work in Progress, Save for Later"

Some students may not complete their projects within the allotted time for student-initiated work. As a result, these students may become frustrated if their important projects are deconstructed or taken home incomplete. Teachers communicate respect for student work by allowing students to save and return to projects over time. By designating a space for ongoing work, teachers allow students to be thoughtful and intentional in their work, using the spot to "hold work" until time allows additional work and exploration. For example, a student working on an elaborate small block house is able to add greater detail over the duration of the week. The complete project provides a clear illustration of the student's emerging awareness of symbolic representation and use of narrative to share a story about the design. This information may have been missed had the time for long-term exploration not been extended.

TK teachers may go about creating a "work in progress" station in a variety of ways:

- Set aside space for work in progress at a level easily accessible to the student.
  - » Use a small table in a protected area, away from high-traffic zones.
  - » Repurpose program furnishings such as cubby units or shelf tops.
  - » Provide small trays that are stored in different locations.
- Label designated surfaces with a sign (e.g., "Work in Progress, Save for Later") to promote community care and respect.
- For limited space or popular materials, take digital photos to serve as a blueprint for use at a later time when a material or activity is made available again.

Ideas for Supporting Additional Accommodations for Learning
(Sadao and Robinson 2010; Isbell and Isbell 2005)

Tangram Blocks: Provide tangrams that have raised lines to further shape distinction through touch; outline with highlighter pen or tape.

Pattern Stamps: Use a sponge roller to cover the stamp handle to make it easier for children to grip and stamp images.

Puzzles: Add wooden doorknob grippers to puzzle pieces.

Student Journals: Provide a picture cue attached to words. Use real pictures of activities. Use a speech-generating device such as talking picture cards or talking photo albums to reinforce a link between picture, word, and sound. Use an electronic tablet drawing application to expose the student to creating pictures by selecting predrawn symbols; use a story sequencing application to add real pictures to a journal story instead of drawing a picture.

Homemade Books: Make baggie books with added Velcro on each baggie page for three-dimensional props to be added.

Adapted Books: Add colored highlighter tape over color words that correspond to the color of the tape and add white correction tape to cover cluttered backgrounds and wordy descriptions.

Stabilized Materials: Use textured shelf liner under toys and games to secure them to tables; use self-sticking fabric strips to fasten items to a table or tray.

invite students to work from a place of comfort and familiarity (Copple and Bredekamp, 2009; Epstein 2007; Riley et al. 2008). Additionally, educators can plan for integrated learning experiences within learning areas to maximize learning during student-initiated work. One way to achieve this goal is to incorporate props and materials aimed at promoting literacy learning.

In the next section, recommendations are made for supplying learning areas in the TK classroom. This general list is meant to serve as a starting place for program planning, not as an exhaustive list. Initially, TK teachers may not have access to all materials, and they may need to acquire supplies over time. High-quality early learning environments are created through intentional planning, implementation, and evaluation. Program design is a reflective process; the classroom space will evolve over time as the teacher grows in his or her professional knowledge and practice and as students' needs change. TK teachers are encouraged to use observations of student work and emerging interests as points of inspiration in program planning and in the continuous development of learning areas throughout the school year. Teachers are encouraged to rotate materials in the TK classroom as new areas of focus present themselves in students' independent and collaborative work.

The **Construction Area** is a space where students plan, solve problems, and participate in individual or group building projects. Ideally, this area should include the following items/materials:

- Wood unit blocks

- Variety of other blocks of varying shapes and sizes (e.g., small unit blocks, large wooden blocks, cardboard brick blocks)

- Materials to extend and support construction play (e.g., plastic people, animals, traffic signs, cars)

- Materials to integrate literacy learning (e.g., books, pencils, clipboards with paper, graph paper)

Promoting a Literacy-Rich Environment

Students are active explorers of their environment; they construct meaning from hands-on learning experiences. To capitalize on students' innate curiosity, educators can structure classrooms in ways that give students numerous opportunities to explore and engage in literacy experiences (National Research Council 2001). TK teachers can take the following actions to support language and literacy development:

- Prepare a Language and Literacy Area with a variety of writing tools, instruments, and paper (e.g., paper or whiteboard) to encourage students to communicate their ideas and experiences and build competencies in letter and word knowledge.

- Supply all other learning areas with portable writing surfaces (e.g., clipboards), paper, and pencils. The intentional placement of writing materials throughout the classroom eliminates "wait time" and traveling across the classroom to collect materials. It also supports the spontaneity that is inherent in student-initiated learning. A student may want to record a recipe in the Dramatic Play Area or create a sign to label a block creation.

- Display environmental print, such as food containers, signs, and literacy artifacts (e.g., newspapers), in conjunction with learning themes to introduce print concepts and encourage students to stop and practice reading skills (Smith 2001).

- Incorporate books related to learning-area content, such as a book about insects in the Science and Discovery Area, books in the Dramatic Play Area that provide students with scripts for play, and literature in the Construction Area and Art Area that inspires crafting and creating.

By supplying the spaces with opportunities to read and write, teachers encourage student-initiated learning and promote playful encounters with literacy. Adult interactions with students will enhance these spontaneous learning experiences. During students' choice time, teachers can circulate around the classroom, promoting the incorporation of these resources to expand children's learning (Epstein 2007). For example, a teacher may sketch a block structure on paper and then invite students to label their blueprint. Program or parent volunteers may provide support in a literacy-rich environment. Encourage volunteers to model reading and writing skills such as demonstrating the use of coupons or writing a grocery list in the Dramatic Play Area food market. Adult presence adds new depth, meaning, and fun to students' initiated play themes.

The **Reading Area** is intended for individual or small-group exploration of storybooks, as well as rest and reflection. Ideally include the following items/materials:

- Variety of books and magazines related to current theme/topic
- Soft/cozy materials (e.g., carpet, bean bags, pillows)
- Comfortable seating (e.g., child-size couch, rocking chair)

The **Listening Area** is planned to promote independent exploration of book reading and print concepts. Ideally, the following items should be included in this area:

- Audio player
- Multiple sets of headphones with docking stations
- Chairs (which may include beanbag chairs)
- Audiobooks (or books with accompanying recordings)

Choosing Quality Books

Storybook reading has an important impact on long-term language and literacy development. For young children, book reading provides experience with vocabulary, exposure to the cadences of written language, an introduction to the structure of stories, and opportunities for sustained attention (Justice and Pullen 2003; Wells 2009). Research has also found that children who have access to numerous, high-quality books show competencies in narration, concepts of print, concepts of writing, and letter knowledge (Jalongo 2004). The California Reading Task Force suggests that each classroom have access to a minimum of 1,500 books (CDE 1999) of various types. This recommendation includes books stored in the school library and does not mean that all books have to be displayed in the classroom at the same time. A classroom's collection of books should include the following types:

- Literature (fiction)
- Informational text (nonfiction)
- Picture books illustrated with drawings, paintings, and photos
- Folk storybooks
- Concept books (e.g., alphabet books, color and shape books, counting books, and so forth)
- Predictable books
- Poetry books
- Riddle and joke books
- Children's magazines
- Homemade and student-made books
- Photo albums of the students

Choosing Quality Books *(continued)*

Classroom libraries can include a wide variety of books that reflect the diverse make-up of the classroom and the cultural and ethnic diversity of the school community. This includes:

- Books showing people of all races, ages, and physical abilities
- Books reflecting experiences of single-parent, two-parent, and extended families
- Books in the home language of the students
- Books with female and male main characters

The books made available to students may be rotated throughout the year according to themes and emerging projects. Although a quiet, comfortable space designated for reading is important, books should be displayed throughout the classroom. Provide books that share information and connect and expand on play themes. For example, displaying a book about different types of buildings in the Construction Area may inspire students to build a skyscraper or learn the names of the different machines used to construct such towers. Selecting high-quality books for lesson planning is also important. When choosing narrative texts for shared-book reading, educators can consider the following (Jalongo 2004):

- Characterization: Are the characters memorable and portrayed well?
- Plot: Does the book present a sequence of events that are interesting and understandable to students?
- Settings: Are settings portrayed accurately in informational books and imaginatively in literature books?
- Use of language: Is the language concrete and vivid? Is the language easy to follow?
- Quality of art and design: Do the illustrations capture the reader's attention?
- Interplay between pictures and words: Do the illustrations enrich the story? Do they move the story forward? Do they enhance the meaning, establish the mood, or clarify information in the story?

It is important to provide informational texts in learning areas and on reading shelves, but it is equally important to expose children to shared reading experiences with informational text. Barbara Moss (2003) suggests looking for the 5 A's when selecting engaging informational books:

- Authority: The author presents information on the topic with authority
- Accuracy: The author ensures the accuracy of the information
- Attractiveness: The book has "kid appeal"
- Appropriateness: The content is appropriate for the age level
- Artistry: The text is clearly organized, interesting, and written in a way that children can understand and enjoy

(From *Exploring the Literature of Fact: Children's Nonfiction Trade Books in the Elementary Classroom*, by Barbara Moss. See References section for further information.)

The **Language and Literacy Area** supports the development of letter knowledge, fine-motor control, and emergent writing skills. To match all students' personal writing styles and skills, a wide range of materials is encouraged and needed. Ideally, the following items should be included in the Language and Literacy Area:

- Many types of paper (e.g., construction paper, lined/unlined paper, tracing paper, journals, envelopes)

- Many varieties of writing instruments (e.g., pens, pencils, markers, crayons, colored pencils, chalkboard, whiteboard)

- Word books or cards (in English and the home language(s) of students in the class)

- Letter-making tools (e.g., letter stamps, stickers, and stencils)

- Adaptive writing instruments and writing surfaces

- Picture dictionary, sight word rings, and/or word wall with students' names and other words relevant to themes and activities

- Manufactured or homemade listening tubes

- Alphabet strips (visual and tactile)

- Literacy games (e.g., alphabet bingo, phoneme match, story sequencing)

- Books with letters, letter sounds, and simple text

The **Art Area** fosters creative expression, reasoning skills, and integrated learning. It is designed to support student-initiated work as well as teacher-directed experiences. A variety of tools, loose items, and consumables can be made available to students each day. Projects that promote new skills or expose students to different media and cultural works could also be incorporated over time. Ideally, the following items should be included in the Art Area:

- Easel station

- Paper (e.g., construction, textured, plain)

- Paint (e.g., watercolor, tempera, and a variety of paint colors)

- Pencils, markers, crayons, colored pencils, and a variety of crayon colors

- Collage materials

- Scissors, glue, glue sticks, clear tape, colored tape

- Modeling clay and dough

- Sculpting tools

- Recyclables (e.g., toilet paper tubes, strawberry baskets, plastic bottles)

- Miscellaneous project supplies

- Name cards to support writing

- Books about artists from different parts of the world, mixed media, and "how-to" crafts

The **Computer Area** is dedicated to introducing students to technology through age-appropriate software and adaptive keyboards and instruments. Ideally, the following items should be included in this area:

- Computers with two seats each (to encourage cooperative learning)
- Child-friendly hardware, such as oversized keyboards, colored keyboard keys, a mouse, and touch screens
- Headphones
- Developmentally appropriate educational software and Web sites
- Picture cues for visual instruction of computer use

The **Science and Discovery Area** is a space designed to encourage students to explore, ask questions, and pursue answers through the inquiry process. Specific investigations can vary over time

and incorporate a regular selection of science tools to match emerging topics of study. Ideally, the following items should be included in the Science and Discovery Area:

- Science tools (e.g., magnifying lenses, rulers, color shields, scales, mirrors, tweezers, pipettes, and so forth)
- Activities that change over time (e.g., magnets, insects, seasons, life cycles)
- Living things (e.g., plants and classroom pets)
- Pencils
- Clipboards with paper
- Science concept books

The **Math and Manipulatives Area** promotes conceptual learning of numbers, shapes, attributes, patterns, and mathematical reasoning. Many of the materials supplied in this learning area also build fine-motor strength. Ideally, the following items should be included in this area:

- A wide variety of math manipulatives (e.g., counting bears, Unifix cubes, pattern links, tangram shapes)
- Number strips
- Math tools (e.g., rulers, sorting tubs or mats, scales)
- Pencils
- Graph paper
- Clipboards with paper

- Collections of objects for counting, sorting, and pattern making (e.g., buttons, seeds, keys, old crayons)

- Puzzles

- Math games (e.g., board games, dice, number bingo)

- Books that focus on math concepts

The **Sensory Area** invites students to pursue experiences that concentrate on developing and engaging the five senses. This can be a messy exploration, so TK teachers may consider placing this area in the outdoor learning environment if possible. Table-top adaptations may also be incorporated to work with limited space. Ideally, the following items should be included in the Sensory Area:

- Modeling clay

- Dry goods (e.g., packing peanuts, natural materials, beads, textiles)

- Sand

- Water

- Spill and fill containers

- Small pieces for dramatic play (e.g., dollhouse furniture, plastic people, small animals)

Supplying the Space

TK students are best supported when programs incorporate child-size tables, dramatic play areas, and open-ended manipulatives and construction supplies (e.g., blocks, recyclables). Although some school districts may have funds set aside for initial start-up, others work with limited budgets. Teachers of young children are known for their resourcefulness; they can find uses for discarded furniture and know how to pick out valuable items at garage sales. They also know how to generate community support and donations. The following are additional ideas for supplying the TK classroom:

- Work with school and district administrators to determine additional funding opportunities for the TK program.

- Borrow within the classroom/school community.

- Get assistance to seek and apply for local, regional, and national grants.

- Salvage kindergarten equipment that is no longer in use.

- Post a wish list of materials for parents and families to donate. The list should include free goods (e.g., computers donated from a workplace or recyclables from home) as well as items of different price ranges.

- Create and collect homemade materials and curriculum supplies (e.g., felt stories, modeling clay, old buttons, muffin tins, matching games).

- Make use of professional colleagues' expertise; visit Web sites that offer free songs and activities.

The **Dramatic Play Area** is collaborative in nature and should be well stocked to promote positive peer interaction and cooperative learning experiences. Vocabulary development and conceptual knowledge will be promoted by varying the learning themes in this area. Initially, the following items should be included in the Dramatic Play Area:

- Table, chairs, and other furniture (e.g., kitchen set)
- Play food and empty food containers
- Telephone (and a phone book)
- Dress-up clothes (e.g., everyday clothes and fantasy)
- Diversity dolls
- Baskets, woven fabrics, and images from different home experiences
- Variety of props and costumes to rotate over time
- Literacy props and artifacts
- Puppet theatre and puppets
- Pencils, clipboard with paper
- Theme-related books

Space for Families

The home–school partnership contributes significantly to student achievement outcomes (National Coalition for Parent Involvement in Education [NCPIE] 2006). Family involvement

Dramatic Play— Going Beyond the Kitchen

Dramatic play is a valuable component of a student's educational experience; it is collaborative in nature and presents opportunities for using language and developing everyday math and social-studies skills. Students explore numbers as they set the correct number of plates for dinner, practice reading as they decode the text on an empty food container, and share their knowledge of community helpers as they care for sick babies. Teachers should consider moving beyond a traditional arrangement of the Dramatic Play Area, which typically includes a play kitchen, table and chairs, doll bed, and a storage area for dress-up clothes. Although this design offers many valuable learning experiences, teachers can do much to extend students' educational play:

- Supply prop boxes with a variety of realia. For example, a veterinary hospital prop box may include doctors' tool kits, stuffed animals, soft bandages, copies of animal x-rays, patient files, veterinarian scrubs, and appointment books.

- Seek donations from families and community partners to obtain materials that reflect diverse cultures.

- If possible, invite experts to speak to the class about their insights and experiences. These real-world connections may inspire interest in new themes for the dramatic play area.

- Rotate dramatic prop boxes to match current curricular focus.

- Make prop boxes compact to meet classroom storage needs.

is positively associated with peer friendship skills, academic success, school attendance, and motivation to succeed. In this document, the terms families and parents are used interchangeably to refer to the significant caretakers in a student's life. These terms include but are not limited to biological family relations, adoptive or foster parents, and other individuals who may not be related to the children in their care.

TK teachers can utilize many strategies for establishing and maintaining authentic partnerships with parents—and the program environment may be instrumental in this process (Nagel and Wells 2009). Designating space for families is an important part of program design. A family communication board can be used for postings related to educational routines, school updates, and current curriculum. Information related to volunteer opportunities can be displayed in attractive formats to attract the attention of parents.

Displaying Student Work

Students take great pride in their work. Although some students prefer to take important projects home, many enjoy seeing their artwork, writing, or models on display in the classroom. Families, too, relish the opportunity to see tangible evidence of their children's learning displayed throughout the classroom environment. Children's positive sense of self is nurtured when they see that important adults, teachers, and families have noticed their efforts. Furthermore, classroom displays of meaningful work create a sense of community, and they are a source of inspiration for future projects. For these reasons, TK teachers should designate functional space for classroom displays, which should be placed at the students' eye level so that children will have easy access to their work. Permanent displays, those used for a uniform purpose over time (e.g., a Science Area Investigations magnet board), could be combined with portable displays (e.g., moveable picture frames or raised platforms for model display)

to promote ease of use and documentation throughout the early learning environment. Magnets on metal cabinets and masking tape for walls invite students to take part in the creation of displays. Documentation of student work could include both student-initiated work as well as items representative of small-group and large-group learning experiences.

It is common for teachers to include every piece of work generated in group activities. However, this can lead to cluttered walls and an emphasis on uniform, product-based work. TK teachers may choose to display work in this fashion or perhaps consider highlighting unique individual work—projects that reveal each student's unique strengths and interests. Changing displays of work periodically ensures that each student is represented and shows a progression in development over time. Teachers and students may also choose to co-create program displays that draw attention to community learning experiences, such as field trips (e.g., Our Visit to the Post Office) and cooperative projects (e.g., Our Community Garden). It may take time for families to adjust to the new format of a display, but when teachers explain the purpose and send home other important work, families will likely value the investment in reflecting individuality and promoting community efforts.

Extending Learning from the Classroom to the Outdoor Environment

Many activities that originate in the indoor classroom can be extended into the outdoor environment. The programs should emphasize real experiences for students. As an illustration, an activity that explores the changing of seasons might document the change in a neighborhood or play yard tree over time. Active learning in outdoor spaces will engage students differently than experiences constructed and executed in

Planning for Physical Education

Educators make use of outdoor environments to plan learning experiences that are specifically designed to engage students in gross-motor activities and coordinated movement. Open-ended gross-motor play invites students to practice movement skills, but "some structuring of physical activity is necessary to help children maximize their movement experiences" (Sanders 2002, 31). Organized gross-motor games,

such as Red Light, Green Light or Teacher, May I, promote the development of large-motor muscle control, balance, and complex, integrated movement. These combined skills are put to use in a variety of everyday tasks such as moving across a space, jumping and landing, and writing and drawing. It is important for all students to have opportunities to develop and practice specific and varied forms of physical movement. These movement experiences influence the specific gross- and fine-motor skills children will be able to perform as they grow and participate in more organized sports and physical activities. TK teachers have the opportunity to expose students to a variety of movement skills (e.g., galloping, skipping, hopping) and help them build control and competence in the early years.

To plan an effective physical education curriculum, educators need to be knowledgeable about the diverse movement skills and the specific developmental sequence of these skills. Resources such as the *California Preschool Learning Foundations, Volume 2* (CDE 2010b), and the *California Preschool Curriculum Framework, Volume 2* (CDE 2011), offer clear definitions of different areas of physical development, descriptions of development, and examples of skills in real contexts. Furthermore, the

framework provides specific materials and activities that are designed to engage students in active play and promote coordinated action. Additionally, *The Intentional Teacher: Choosing the Best Strategies for Young Children's Learning* (Epstein 2007) details both child-initiated and adult-initiated play experiences that facilitate physical development.

the indoor classroom. Teachers are encouraged to reflect on indoor learning experiences and consider whether the activity might be better implemented in an outdoor setting.

Dramatic play is an activity that easily extends to outdoor play. In the school play yard, students can be observed engaging in pretend adventures or recreating plots or themes from media as well as real life. TK teachers can encourage this form of

creative expression by providing students with the tools and props to dramatize their stories. Old play kitchen bowls, cups, and utensils invite students to "cook" using natural materials (e.g., grass, leaves, and rocks) from the play yard. Dress-up clothes help students transform into pretend play characters. Just as the indoor dramatic play area can be transformed over time, so too can the outdoor dramatic play props. Camping, firefighter play, and superheroes are all possible extensions

Benefiting Hearts and Minds

As the world becomes increasingly virtual and children's everyday experiences become infused with technology (e.g., computers, television, cellular phones), real encounters with the natural world become ever more important. Many young children have limited opportunities to engage with their natural world because they live their lives largely indoors (Louv 2005). Some families keep their children inside for safety reasons, while others do not live near green spaces that are natural for play (Rivkin 1995). Given this trend, concerns have been raised in relation to childhood obesity and mental health (Louv 2005). Although children present their symptoms differently, they—like adults—experience stress as a result of the fast-paced world in which they live. Recent attention has been drawn to the positive social–emotional outcomes associated with time spent in outdoor play spaces.

Much of social–emotional development takes place in the contexts of relationships. The open-ended context of outdoor spaces naturally lends itself to promoting authentic connections with peers and adults (Thompson and Thompson 2007) in the following ways:

- As students organize games, partake in dramatic play adventures, and resolve conflicts, they are practicing skills (e.g., negotiation, leadership, collaboration) that will be used throughout their personal and communal life.

- Time spent in natural spaces offers student's opportunities to slow down, reflect, and simply enjoy the moment. Research has shown that "as little as four minutes in a garden will start to reduce stress, improve mood, and stead the vital signs" (Nature Explore 2011).

- Student-initiated challenges in outdoor environments permit students to push their limits and build self-awareness of their strengths and emerging abilities.

- The natural world evokes students' sense of wonder. Curiosity and creativity are nurtured as students look under rocks, collect seed pods, and blow apart the blossoms of dandelion weeds.

Spending time in outdoor spaces gives students the opportunity to practice behaviors that nurture relationships and promote kindness and gentleness (Rosenow 2008). TK teachers who attend to these acts of care and comment on the positive impact on others reinforce positive attitudes and nurturing actions.

of students' interest in role-play experiences. To promote ease of use, prop boxes should be placed near the area where children will play. For example, if preparing a "gas station," consider setting dramatic play props near the bike path/area.

TK students benefit from regular time and exposure to the open-ended context of the outdoor play yard. Through individual exploration, cooperative play, and collaborative investigation, the outdoor environment promotes the development of self-regulation, a positive sense of self, peer play skills, and focused attention (Thompson and Thompson 2007). Additionally, outdoor spaces are rich in academic learning (Nature Explore 2011) as real science, environmental print, and exposure to shapes and patterns are some of the opportunities present in the school play yard. Programs vary in terms of the physical landscape, natural resources, and outdoor curriculum materials. Although a site might lack traditional "green" space, all programs can enhance students' learning experiences by making use of the outdoor environment.

The school play yard has traditionally been used by educators to give students an opportunity for unstructured activity. Recess is a time for connecting with peers, climbing on equipment that promotes the development of gross-motor skills, and participating in student-organized games. Young children need to engage in active play. Adults may view this type of play as off-task for educational settings, but research speaks to the significance of such integrated movement in a child's development. Physical activity provides students with important health benefits, but it has also been associated with positive outcomes in social skills and learning (CDE 2013b). Students who regularly participate in active movement are alert and ready to learn. Although it is important for teachers to plan and implement structured physical movement aimed at refining gross-motor muscle control, balance, and eye–hand coordination (see the highlight on planning for physical education on the next page), research also highlights the value of student-initiated movement and opportunities for unstructured gross-motor play.

Outdoor areas are sometimes more difficult to modify in order for all children to experience play. Using UDL to explore whether changes to the outdoor environment can be implemented may help adjust access to areas typically not available to children with motor and other developmental delays. For instance, simply adding blocks to pedals on tricycles with self-sticking fabric straps attached may allow a child with ambulatory issues a chance to ride a bike. A wagon is another possible alternative to bike riding, offering a child who is unable to pull the vehicle the opportunity to participate as a passenger. Sometimes, slides and swings are located in an area that creates barriers for wheelchairs and children who are unable to manage stairs. A potential solution might be to take pictures of the outdoor areas (such as the slides) and create a visual scene of the place. A child in a wheelchair is then equipped with a voice output device that says "Go!"

to make a request for children to go down the slide. Children then slide, one at a time, upon hearing the command. The child may not be on the slide but is participating in the activity by calling out the directions and pointing to the visual scene depiction of the event. The visual scene helps spark interest in the activity, especially when children see themselves in the picture.

Outdoor play offers children with disabilities an opportunity to interact with other students in a safe and fun learning atmosphere. Outdoor play is an appropriate time to work on following directions and transitioning from one activity to the next when following typical daily routines pose challenges for some students. The unstructured nature of outdoor play enhances students' positive peer interactions and freedom to express themselves around events they enjoy.

Supplying the Space

Much like the TK classroom, the outdoor environment can include spaces for focused learning. There are portable, flexible options for incorporating structured encounters into daily outdoor learning. For example, rather than a stationary Writing Area, TK teachers can create transportable writing bags or writing suitcases. A tote bag or small suitcase supplied with a notepad, pencil box, and alphabet/word cards invites students to document their ideas, write a letter to a family member, or simply sketch an image.

Experiences from the Science and Discovery Area can also be easily introduced into the outdoor space. The outdoor classroom is naturally inclusive of real science explorations. To go beyond casual observations, students need science tools to focus and quantify their observations (Twibell and Harkins, forthcoming). Simple activities such as taking a closer look at a crawling insect or examining a pod from a towering tree encourage students to practice the inquiry skills used by scientists. Additional ideas for practice may be

How to Make an Outdoor Science Kit

Promote the development of inquiry skills by providing students with readily accessible science kits during outdoor curriculum time, recess, and field work experiences. Introduce the kits during a large-group meeting to highlight vocabulary and use. Provide opportunities for students to practice immediately after the group meeting to reinforce conceptual learning.

Materials Needed

- Plastic tote or pail, labeled "Science Kit"
- Magnifying lens
- Tweezers
- Ruler
- Empty plastic containers (e.g., petri dishes, film canisters, bug jars, small sorting bins)
- Clipboards with paper
- Writing instruments (e.g., gently used pencils, pens, crayons from indoor classroom)
- Specific learning-theme items (e.g., bug net, mirror, envelopes for collecting pods)

reviewed in the *California Preschool Learning Foundations, Volume 3* (CDE 2013b), and the *California Preschool Curriculum Framework, Volume 3* (CDE 2013a).

Planting a Seed for Change

Educational settings can promote children's active engagement with nature. Not all programs have expansive lawns or established trees, so programs with those types of limitations need to embrace creative, collaborative thinking as well as short- and long-term planning. Long-term planning could involve partnering with local, regional, and national organizations aimed at improving outdoor spaces for children. For example, the National Arbor Day Foundation collaborates on the Dimensions Project, a nationwide initiative to build Nature Explore Classrooms for early childhood programs and elementary school settings. Short-term solutions may also engage community partners, but they are often quick in planning and simple in execution. For example, a short-term activity may be the planting of a small tree in the ground or in a wooden barrel that has wheels for portability. Small garden beds or boxes can house plants or simple produce to promote health education and food science. Programs with limited funds can still plan nature explorations, no matter how insignificant those experiences may appear to be. Examples include bird watching, tracking a squirrel as it searches for food, or scouting for ants. These activities, and others like them, have value and promote real connections with the natural world.

Summary

High-quality learning environments include outdoor settings where students are actively engaged. Tools that assess program quality may offer guidance and standardized descriptors of high-quality learning environments. Some tools evaluate physical space, others examine teacher–student interactions and instructional strategies, and additional tools assess both environment and educational interactions. Although TK teachers are not required to assess their program design and practices, doing so may lead to a deeper understanding of best practices and offer insights into program strengths and opportunities for improvement (Sugarman 2011).

The TK classroom should be supplied with a variety of materials that are rotated over time. With a number of learning areas and materials, a designated area for storage should be identified for these resources. Creative solutions range from consolidated legal boxes to attractive baskets on top of permanent cabinets. Easy access ensures efficient program preparation and supports emergent learning.

A well-designed TK environment that offers structured choice and extends learning to outdoor spaces does much to invite and engage students in the learning process. Integrated learning opportunities further extend conceptual learning and promote real uses of reading and writing. Through careful observation and thoughtful reflection, teachers plan learning experiences that match current student inquiry and curricular goals.

CHAPTER 6
Assessment and Differentiated Instruction in the Transitional Kindergarten Classroom

Assessment and Differentiated Instruction in the Transitional Kindergarten Classroom
http://www4.scoe.net/ims/webcasts/cf/index.
cfm?fuseaction=archivedDetail&eventID=140&archiveID=255

Assessment and Differentiated Instruction in the Transitional Kindergarten Classroom
(YouTube with Captions)
http://www.youtube.com/watch?v=B73fPXrK9xM

To effectively support student learning, educators need to use appropriate assessment tools and data to differentiate instruction and communicate with families about students' progress. This chapter includes four sections. The first section, An Overview of Transitional Kindergarten Assessment, discusses the basics of TK assessment, including the need to ensure that assessments are developmentally appropriate, aligned with their stated purposes, and administered over time and in a variety of settings. The first section also provides suggestions for collecting and organizing assessment data. The second section, Response to Instruction and Intervention in the Transitional Kindergarten Program, provides information about RtI[2] and highlights the importance of effective ongoing assessment in monitoring student progress and providing appropriate tiered intervention based on students' needs. The third section, Using Evidence from Assessment to Differentiate Instruction, provides additional information about and strategies for differentiating instruction to meet the assessed needs of children. The final section, Communicating with Families About Student Learning, concludes the chapter with suggestions for sharing information about student progress with families.

An Overview of Transitional Kindergarten Assessment

Assessment is used in schools to support learning, monitor student progress, differentiate instruction, communicate with other teachers and families, identify students with disabilities, and evaluate and examine program trends (Jones 2004). This section discusses several areas for educators to consider when designing and implementing a TK assessment plan:

- Developmentally Appropriate Assessments
- Assessments with Specific Purposes
  - » Formal Assessments
  - » Informal Assessments
- Assessments Administered Over Time and in a Variety of Contexts
- Collecting, Organizing, and Reviewing Evidence from Assessments

Assessments are conducted both formally and informally depending on the stated, intentional goals for learning. The use of ongoing, multiple measures of student progress to support learning and to inform instruction practice is discussed.

Vignette

It is Ms. Gengler's first time teaching in a TK classroom. As she prepares for the school year ahead, she is filled with excitement and a little anxiety; she is concerned with how she will monitor student learning. Although she is certain she will make use of observation and work samples from student portfolios, Ms. Gengler will also supplement her informal measures with other standardized assessment tools. Ms. Gengler is preparing for a meeting with a school administrator and other TK/K colleagues in the district. The meeting will focus on reviewing a variety of assessment tools for the TK classroom. During the review, they will need to examine the tools carefully, looking at the purpose and use of assessment in the TK classroom. Are the tools developmentally appropriate? Can they be conducted using authentic assessment? What areas of learning do the tools monitor? Will the tools be culturally and linguistically appropriate for all of Ms. Gengler's TK students? What professional development will be required to use the tools accurately? In preparation for her meeting, Ms. Gengler decides to print a list of assessment tools to consider. She is certain that, with the help of the administrator and input from colleagues, she will be able to make a clear and thorough plan for assessing what students are learning in her TK classroom.

Developmentally Appropriate Assessments

In response to the developmental needs of young learners, the format of TK assessments differs from methods used in later school experiences. TK students are concrete learners who are in the process of developing their oral language and fine-motor skills (Gullo 2006). Assessments for TK learners should be informal, authentic, and strength-based (CCSESA 2011). Shillady (2004) defines assessment as a process of discovering children's abilities as it relates to optimal development and program goals. Teachers can use this information to plan appropriate curriculum and instructional strategies. Developmentally, TK students are diverse; they vary in terms of maturation and experiential background. "Sound assessment of young children is challenging because they develop and learn in ways that are characteristically uneven and embedded within the specific cultural and linguistic contexts in which they live" (Copple and Bredekamp 2009, 22).

The varied development of TK students contributes to the challenge of monitoring their learning to ensure that they are progressing toward the expected outcomes that will enable them to successfully meet or exceed standards by the end of the second year in kindergarten. According to Copple and Bredekamp (2009), developmentally appropriate assessment of children's progress:

- is ongoing, strategic, and purposeful;

- focuses on student growth toward goals based on assessed needs;

- includes a system for collecting and reflecting on information that is used to plan curriculum and learning experiences;

- uses appropriate and individualized methods to assess learning and provides varied opportunities for students to demonstrate competency;

- provides information about what students are able to accomplish independently with the assistance of adults or other children;

- incorporates information from families and from the children themselves;

- is designed for a specific purpose and used only as intended;

- includes information from multiple sources when decisions such as placement have a major impact on students;

- always includes appropriate follow-up, evaluation, and referral if there is an indication that a child may have a special learning or developmental need.

Effective teachers are decision makers; they observe, reflect, and respond to student needs by creating detailed lesson plans that provide guidance about what to teach and how to teach. Developmentally appropriate assessments inform TK instruction as teachers monitor each student's knowledge, skills, and interests.

Assessments with Specific Purposes

Educators need to carefully evaluate their assessment requirements and select assessments that will provide the information they need. Assessment strategies lie on a continuum from formal to informal (National Institute for Early Education Research 2004). Educators who are clear about the purpose and value of assessment consistently use both formal and informal tools to ensure a successful learning experience for all students. TK teachers are conscious of learning standards as they assess student learning and student progress over time. Data gathered from informal and formal assessment tools shapes teacher support, highlighting the specific skills and concepts that need additional instruction or reinforcement. This information is used to conceptualize individual and group learning experiences (Heroman and Copple 2006).

Formal Assessments

Formal, summative assessments might include criteria-based readiness tests, screening tools, diagnostic developmental instruments, standards-based achievement tests, or other reliable and valid tools. Formal assessments are administered periodically, annually, or during defined benchmark periods. Careful consideration needs to be given to the effective use of standardized assessment tools in the TK classroom. Standardized assessment tools provide important information about student knowledge and skills, but they are selected with attention to the nature and use of the specific tool. According to Shillady (2004), school administrators and TK teachers may want to select a standardized assessment tool that has the following characteristics:

- Developmentally appropriate for TK students

- Reliably assesses all areas of learning

- Uses multiple measures and includes diverse forms of data collected in a variety of contexts

- Used after professional development (where necessary) to ensure fidelity of implementation

- Accurately assesses all learners (the tool is culturally and linguistically appropriate and includes accommodations for children with disabilities)

- Used to inform instruction and curriculum planning

- Supports student progress toward meeting state standards

Informal Assessments

At the informal end of the assessment continuum, approaches might include observation notes, student work collections, parent surveys, and other information about student progress. In general, informal assessments reflect authentic learning experiences, are conducted much more frequently, and are often more representative of student knowledge over time. Informal assessment is also referred to as *naturalistic* or *authentic* assessment because this method of monitoring student progress and achievement is integrated

into student daily work (Maxwell and Clifford 2004) and is often used to extend and complement more formal assessment. Informal assessments are "formative" in nature because they provide evidence that can be used immediately to "inform" or shape instructional practice. They are embedded in children's daily activities and explorations. Where possible, assessment data should be "collected as part of children's involvement in meaningful activities that relate to real-life situations where children will actually be using the skill" (Jacobs and Crowley 2010, 33). In addition, recording observations of children at work can assist educators to understand the unique skill sets and personalities in their classroom (Dombro, Jablon, and Stetson 2011).

Observation is the core of informal assessment strategies. Evidence of learning may be gathered during student-initiated work or while a student participates in a teacher directed small-group activity. Large-group learning experiences offer TK teachers additional opportunities to assess group learning needs and note differences in individual responses to and understanding of the information presented or discussed. As mentioned above, educators who monitor work in real contexts are better able to assess student knowledge as children represent their ideas, explain concepts, and demonstrate skills. For example, a teacher might assess a student's knowledge of number sense as the child counts spaces on a board game. Watching a student sort a collection of seeds during outside time, taking a picture of a writing sample from a small-group activity, or recording social skills used during snack time all combine to reflect a more holistic view of a child's development. Collecting a wide variety of informal evidence (e.g., noting verbal responses, collecting pictures of visual or symbolic representations, gathering writing samples, making notes about motor skills) helps ensure that each child's interests, skills, competencies, and growth over time are recognized in the assessment process.

Assessments Administered Over Time and in a Variety of Contexts

As discussed in the previous section, both formal and informal assessments are used to monitor student progress. No matter which assessment tools are used, effective educators recognize the need to observe and collect data over time. Young children's learning is episodic; students will vary in what they know and are able to demonstrate at one point in time as opposed to another (Copple and Bredekamp 2009). To capture an accurate and comprehensive picture of each child's development, teachers should use systematic and ongoing assessments. Additionally, the assessment context may influence a student's ability to share

Desired Results Development Profile–School Readiness (DRDP-SR©)

The Desired Results Development Profile-School Readiness (DRDP-SR) was designed for TK and kindergarten teachers to observe student learning and to document progress toward developmentally appropriate academic and social–emotional goals (CDE 2012a). The DRDP-SR instrument was created for four primary purposes:

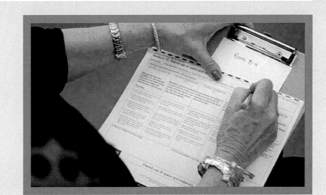

1. As a psychometric measurement of children's development in key domains of school readiness

2. To support the transition between preschool, TK, and kindergarten

3. As a research tool

4. As a professional development resource for teachers

The DRDP-SR encourages teachers to observe and engage with students at work, embedding the assessment process within the curriculum and daily routine. Anecdotal records, student work/portfolios, writing samples, and other evidence of learning are collected over time to generate a progress report of current and emerging skills and abilities. The DRDP-SR instrument is culturally sensitive and linguistically responsive to diverse populations of students. Because the DRDP-SR is a new tool for many professionals, professional development should be provided to promote accuracy of observation and to help eliminate potential rater bias.

and demonstrate his or her knowledge. Like adults, "children may act differently according to the situation" (Jablon, Dombro, and Dichtelmiller 2007, 64). Some students show competence in large-group call-and-response tasks, and others are better equipped to show their knowledge and skills in individual and less-structured tasks. Similarly, some TK children possess the fine-motor control necessary for paper and pencil activities, while others are more comfortable with tasks that utilize manipulatives. To assess students more accurately, teachers can observe and assess in a variety of contexts and offer multiple options for students to demonstrate competence.

Collecting, Organizing, and Reviewing Evidence from Assessments

Even the most experienced educators often feel overwhelmed by the process of data collection, analysis, and use. Although it likely that teachers will modify their assessment plans as the school year unfolds, creating a system for collecting, organizing, and using data is an important first step in the assessment process. To begin, TK teachers create plans for collecting assessment data over time (CDE 2000). Focusing on a set number of students each day, attending to one content area over a period of a week, or underlining specific components of a learning standard in a small- or large-group lesson are options for making assessment a regular part of the daily routine. Easy access to assessment materials and tools is critical; keeping a clipboard with a checklist, sticky paper notes, a notepad, or an observation binder with individual student summary sheets are useful resources to support the TK teacher.

Teachers observe both in the midst of and apart from the action, asking questions to extend and probe for learning (Jablon, Dombro, and Dichtelmiller 2007). Whether the teacher observes from a distance or is actively interacting with a student or a group of students, he or she constantly notices student reactions and performance.

Teachers then record their observations and collect samples of student work to serve as concrete evidence. Evidence from informal assessments can be recorded in many different forms. Ongoing records are generally more detailed, cover longer periods of time, and examine subject-specific skills (e.g., reading). Teacher-made or published checklists are designed to capture discrete skills and knowledge. For example, a teacher may quickly cross off letters as identified by a student in a Letter Bingo game. Digital photos, samples of children's work (e.g., drawings, writing, models), and video or audio recordings also inform teachers of student learning and the efficacy of program practices. Anecdotal records are objective descriptions of a brief moment in time (see highlight on the next page).

After collecting data, educators need a system for organizing and storing notes, work samples, checklists, and summary sheets. TK teachers may choose to create student portfolios or use upright file folder bins or binders. Sorting student work samples by order of date keeps work organized and offers a clear illustration of student development over time. To facilitate program planning, educators can designate a separate space to enter goals for future assessment and to differentiate instruction in lesson plans. Such intentionality provides a clear reminder for teaching and promotes follow-through in data collection. Once collected, assessment data need to be reviewed to shape program design, curriculum planning, and instruction (Dodge et al. 2004). "Too often assessment results are seen as an end product rather than as knowledge that opens the door to learning about each child and to planning meaningful curriculum" (Dodge et al. 2004, 10). Educators who go beyond recording student outcomes take a reflective approach to their practice and note the effect of the environment, instruction, and collaborative relationships on learning. Assessment data are used to identify curricular areas that may require greater development around specific concepts

Documenting Student Learning with Anecdotal Records

Observing students in the natural context of their work and daily routine provides TK teachers with valuable information about student strengths, needs, strategies, and interests. Anecdotal records are written descriptions of a social interaction or student-initiated work. Below is an anecdotal record captured by a teacher:

Erika sat at the Art Area making a "flower book"—a book in which she intended to glue samples of flowers that she would collect. On the cover of the book, she drew a flower. "I want to write 'Flower.' And what is the word that—um, um, um—you can find words inside?" I responded, "Do you mean 'dictionary,' like the one we use at the Writing Area to find the correct spelling of a word?" Erika said, "Yeah! Dictionary! Can you help me write 'Flower Dictionary' here?" I dictated the letters to Erika while she transcribed them onto her book cover.

High-quality anecdotes are defined by the following characteristics (Curtis and Carter 2000):

- Objective in writing style
- Specific; they include all relevant details
- Make use of direct quotes
- Communicate mood where appropriate (e.g., tone of voice, body language, facial expression)
- Complete; they have a beginning, middle, and end

Anecdotes illustrate individual learning and make excellent additions to student portfolios.

and skills. For example, a teacher who finds little evidence of learning in classification skills may choose to modify the TK environment to include more materials to prompt sorting and ordering.

In addition to influencing group goals and objectives for learning, assessment outcomes are used to differentiate instruction to meet individual needs. Individual instruction can be further informed by discussions with support staff, families, and other collaborative partners. Group reflection can facilitate the interpretation and use of assessment data to create individualized plans for learning.

Summary

School administrators and TK teachers have many options when selecting and implementing assessments. As professionals select multiple measures that align with their program design, it is important for them to have well-defined learning goals for students and a clear understanding of the purposes of student and program evaluation. The coordinated use of both formal and informal assessment ensures a more accurate evaluation of student progress. Professional development supports appropriate selection, accurate assessment practices, and reinforces the use of assessment data in program planning. Accurate student evaluation is contingent upon school staff matching assessment objectives with developmentally appropriate practice. Students are assessed throughout the year, in a variety of contexts, and through both formal and informal tools. Settling into a workable assessment routine takes time, but the invested effort is well worth the positive student learning outcomes and program success. TK teachers are better able to meet group and individual goals for learning when they routinely assess the effectiveness of their curriculum and instruction. Individual teacher reflection paired with collaborative discussion also assists in the interpretation of assessment data and facilitates the planning for differentiated instruction. Additional information about differentiated instruction is provided in the next two sections.

Response to Instruction and Intervention in the Transitional Kindergarten Program

Response to Instruction and Intervention (RtI^2) is a recognized strategic instructional model that has gained momentum in K–12 education and has more recently been introduced to programs prior to kindergarten. The key premise behind RtI^2 is providing high-quality, researched-based instruction and behavioral supports for all children, with an emphasis on assessment information that guides more focused teaching and specialized curriculum: "The key features of this approach generally involve gathering information on students' skills to help teachers plan and organize instruction, providing evidenced-based interventions and supports, and monitoring student progress in learning" (NPDCI 2012, 1). RtI^2 enhances instructional practices by organizing them around three tiers of consideration, from least intensive to most intensive interventions, depending on the specific needs of the student as determined by available assessment data. The following vignette highlights how RtI^2 provides an instructional framework for a TK classroom.

Multi-tiered Systems of Support

The Response to Intervention (RtI) model was originally created for implementation in the K–12 field (NCLD 2009; NPDCI 2012). Most recently, the model has been applied to preschool programs and is known as recognition and response (NCLD 2009;

Vignette

Mrs. Carson and Ms. Gomez are busy preparing for their first day co-teaching a fully included TK classroom. Colorful bulletin boards representing curricular themes decorate the room. Students' desks are organized in small groupings around the room with picture labels of students' names and individual reward charts marking each location. The collaborating teachers participated in a two-week RtI2 course over the summer months and are discussing how to implement the three-tiered approach in their new classroom. To inform their initial tiered interventions, they looked at incorporating the formative assessment information that was gathered from previous student screening efforts. They also have planned to gather information from parents at the initial open house and use journaling on a weekly basis to monitor students' progress. They are aware that at Tier 1, they must support all children in the design and presentation of the curriculum. They have already created several small-group intervention plans for students who may need additional practice and information presented using manipulatives and direct instructional methods. They added several individual learning areas (covering various subjects) where follow-up materials on planned curricular themes are available. They know to change approaches in Tier 2 when the assessment information indicates a lack of progress. For a few children who may need accommodations in Tier 3, the teachers are ready with additional supports (a districtwide school study team). They feel confident that their strategies are moving from least to most intensive by using this RtI tiered application in their classroom.

Figure 4: California's Response to Instruction and Intervention (RtI²) Multi-tiered Framework

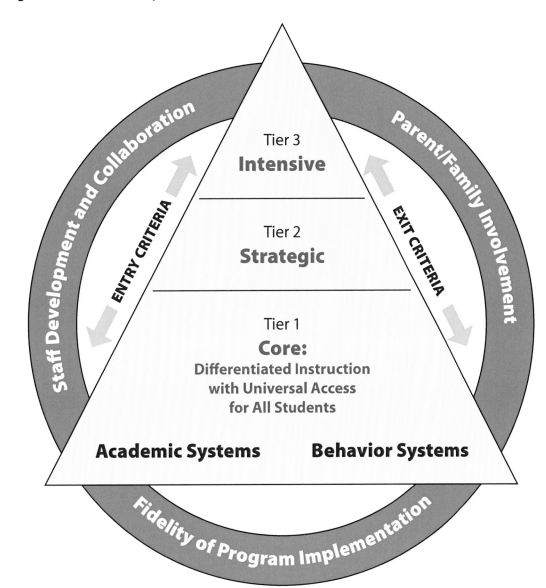

NPDCI 2012). Although not mentioned specifically in law, IDEA 2004 legislation specifies that early intervention services are critical for children who may exhibit the need for additional academic and behavioral supports (DEC, NAEYC, and NHSA 2013). In the current recommendations put forth by the National Center for Learning Disabilities (NCLD), RtI is subsumed under a newer title called Multi-tiered Systems of Support, or MTSS (NCLD 2013). "Multi-tiered Systems of Support programs are referred to globally as Response to Intervention (RtI); however, states and districts may have given

them a local name" (NCLD 2013, 1). MTSS is a relatively new term that encompasses both the RtI models, which typically focus on academics, and the positive behavioral intervention and supports (PBIS) frameworks. These two approaches are often introduced as separate methodologies (Averill and Rinaldi 2011; Gamm et al. 2012). The hallmark of MTSS is the incorporation of evidenced-based techniques, data collection, and problem solving to guide both academic and behavioral interventions. MTSS is now being used to provide an umbrella for both RtI and PBIS considerations. California is

Response to Instruction and Intervention (RtI²)

Tier	Students	Assessment	Curricular Needs	Instruction
1	All (approximately 80% will be successful with generalized curriculum and instruction)	Universal screening and periodic assessment using observation, checklists, curricular measures, and work samples	Evidenced-based general curriculum	Intentional to support all learners
2	Some (approximately 15% will need additional approaches)	Frequent progress monitoring to assess skill acquisition on additional materials	Supplemental activities; repetition	Differentiated for some students who require more support
3	A few (5%)	Assessment of individual skills using additional evaluation tools (both formal and informal); collaborative teaming to identify needs and strategies	An additional curriculum or modifications to the existing materials	Intensive, individualized approaches based on student needs; more time and staff allocated at this level

currently transitioning from RtI² to MTSS, which is a framework that provides a prevention-focused initiative to education by fostering evidence-based practices for all children and employing ongoing student data to adjust curriculum for additional individualization of teaching concepts that particular children may not be grasping. TK teachers are informed of early educational foundations to which students have been exposed in preschool, and they link those concepts with core kindergarten standards. RtI² is well suited to allow TK teachers to embrace early developmental domains of growth—such as early literacy and numeracy, social emotional development,

language, and sensory motor considerations and infuse them into the TK educational goals geared toward more academic skill building.

TK teachers accomplish this integration of developmental factors with academic basics by beginning with the needs of all children at the first tier of instruction and prevent delays in mastery of the subject matter by using assessment information to determine strengths and the need for more targeted instruction at Tier 2. When the efforts made to supplement the instruction with evidenced based materials at tier 2 result in limited student progress, Tier 3 supports are then offered. For instance, a student may begin the school year at grade level as indicated by a screening tool. As the TK teacher administers weekly checklists measuring understanding of the curricular concepts presented, the student demonstrates some gaps in knowledge acquisition. With this progress monitoring information, the TK teacher provides an additional small-group lesson reinforcing previously introduced skills. If the student continues to have difficulty with the subject matter, a tier 3 intervention might be organized that emphasizes increased individualization and additional guided practice and direct teaching strategies.

Important to note is the MTSS/RtI framework is dynamic, not linear in its movement through tiers. Some students may need a tier 3 support in a particular segment of the curriculum and move back to the general curricular area once assessment data shows the student has grasped the particular concept. "Regardless of tier, all teaching and caregiving efforts should be planned and delivered in developmentally appropriate ways that build on children's strengths, interests, and preferences." (DEC, NAEYC, & NHSA, 2013, p.6) Furthermore, a student does not need to be exposed to all three tiers prior to a referral for special education and related services. Paramount to the implementation of the RtI^2 model is the notion of curricular and teaching effectiveness versus the lack of student progress. A change in strategy is warranted when student progress data indicate otherwise.

RtI methodology is a well thought out and planned model incorporating both formative and summative assessment information to guide the ongoing measurement of student progress and success. The features of RtI include: multi-tiered systems of teaching, evidenced based curriculum, ongoing assessment and student progress monitoring, and collaborative problem solving (DEC, NAEYC, NHSA, 2013). By using existing assessment information generated from the DRDPSR and other assessment tools,

TK teachers review student indicators of both academic and behavioral developmental areas to inform instruction. For RtI to be effective, there are several decisions that need to be determined before TK teachers can effectively introduce the model in their classrooms. The most critical considerations are to identify the assessment approaches and critical learning foundations that will be used as guidelines for student progress, choose research-based curricula and subsequent tiered interventions that provide further support to student outcomes, and determine what communication strategies and decision-making rubrics will be employed among teaching staff with families, specialists, and administrators to ensure that decisions are based on relevant data from student assessments (NPDCI 2012).

In 2011, California responded to the charge for implementing RtI in school districts by issuing a document that reviewed the application of the approach on a local level. A team with representatives from the California County Superintendents Educational Services Association (CCSESA), the California Department of Education, and the California Comprehensive Center authored *Response to Instruction and Intervention (RtI^2)—An Implementation and Technical Assistance Guide for Districts and Schools*[*], a document that covers California's version of RtI. The guide focused on K–12 grade levels. In more recent documents, RtI^2 has been renamed MTSS. The purpose of the guide is twofold: to present the basic concepts of RtI (as discussed previously) and to introduce the 10 core components that provide specific features of the RtI approach. The 10 components are as follows:

1. High-quality classroom instruction

2. High expectations

3. Assessments and data collection

4. Problem-solving systems approach

5. Research-based interventions

6. Positive behavioral support

[*]The implementation guide is available at http://cde.ca.gov/ci/cr/ri/ (accessed August 21, 2013)

7. Fidelity of program implementation

8. Staff development and collaboration

9. Parent and family involvement

10. Specific learning disability determination

As shown in figure 4 (see page 91), California's RtI[2] model blends the academic and behavioral approaches under one rubric, which is a defining characteristic of MTSS. Readers are encouraged to explore California's 2011 RtI[2] guide for further information on implementing MTSS/RtI[2] practices in TK classrooms.

Summary

MTSS/RtI is a tiered system of support for TK teachers to reflect upon when designing their overall program plan. MTSS/RtI is a different way of thinking about assessment and intervention that promotes scaffolding of teaching methodologies from less intensive to more intensive approaches directly related to the student assessment outcomes both formative and summative measures. The TK teacher begins with a universal design for learning atmosphere where access to the general education curriculum is assured through thoughtful planning and attention to the learning environment and the instructional delivery. This first step in creating a participatory culture from the start is reflective of Tier 1 in MTSS/RtI. Learning activities and environments are formulated to be safe, engaging, and promote student interest and curiosity. The majority of students are able to demonstrate skill acquisition on universal assessments such as the DRDPSR because TK teachers have determined and instituted UDL strategies at this first tier. If a student is not making adequate and continual progress in developmental skills when presented with the curricular information and daily lesson plans, adjustments are then made by providing differentiated instruction that builds from the student data collected routinely as part of the overall classroom assessment process. This level of the MTSS/RtI pyramid corresponds to

Tier 2. For a very small number of students, Tier 3 supports may be needed to provide additional instructional techniques through targeted curricular modifications and substitutions. The highlight of MTSS/RtI is the bridge between gathering ongoing student progress data that focus on developmental domains and using the information to inform practice and influence teaching efforts based on student success.

Using Evidence from Assessment to Differentiate Instruction

In highly effective programs, TK students have many opportunities to demonstrate their skills and abilities in multiple contexts as they grow and develop. To ensure an accurate and thorough record of students' academic progress, both formal and informal assessments are conducted throughout the year in a wide variety of authentic settings. Teachers thoughtfully and intentionally use evidence from these assessments to plan, implement, and reflect on program curriculum and related instructional activities and to differentiate their instruction to meet the assessed needs of each child. This section reviews the relationship between assessment and differentiated instruction, discusses the need for differentiated instruction, and offers suggestions for implementing differentiated instruction in a TK classroom.

Vignette

Ms. West is monitoring her TK students' progress toward meeting established goals for basic comprehension of both stories and informational books or passages that are read to them. She is reviewing observation notes about student responses during large- and small-group read-aloud sessions and her students' dictated responses to basic comprehension questions. Ms. West notes that most of her students are progressing well and are able to respond to basic questions about the characters, setting, and events of stories and comprehend basic facts presented during shared reading experiences. However, she has noticed that five of her students continue to have difficulty comprehending text and recalling important information that was read and discussed during both large-group and small-group read-aloud sessions. Ms. West decides that she needs additional information. She meets briefly with each student two times over the next week (either during free-choice time or during independent book exploration). During each meeting, which takes approximately two to four minutes, she reads a brief passage that is new to the students (one narrative, one expository) and then engages them in a discussion about the reading. She intentionally embeds a few basic questions in their conversation.

After gathering this additional information, Ms. West learns that two of the five students have adequate comprehension skills when they are focused on the reading. She decides to move them closer to her during read-alouds to make sure she monitors them more closely and engages them more often in discussions. Ms. West also decides that three of the students need additional focused and scaffolded opportunities to listen to text and engage in structured conversations to build their oral comprehension. She decides to continue meeting with the remaining three students in a small group for daily intensive support. She intends to evaluate their progress and determine whether additional differentiation is necessary.

The Need for Differentiated Instruction

As mentioned previously, although the TK cohort is a more chronologically concentrated group than would be found in a traditional kindergarten, there is still significant diversity among the children in terms of their cognitive, social, emotional, linguistic, and physical development. Effective TK teachers are skilled at aligning curriculum content and adjusting instructional strategies with each child's developmental levels and emerging abilities. They "neither underestimate nor overestimate what children can do and learn" (Epstein 2007, 128). TK teachers also intentionally select the most efficient and effective learning setting to introduce new information, reinforce new learning and provide practice opportunities, and/or facilitate discovery and exploration for their students (Copple and Bredekamp 2009, 19).

To ensure an accurate and thorough picture of developmental progress, assessments are conducted throughout the year with data collected from all program activities. Differentiated instruction takes into consideration the variance in abilities across an educational setting. Teachers who understand the complexities of development regularly observe students at work to identify their accomplishments, their readiness for the "next step," and their areas of personal and educational interest (CDE 2000). It is important to note that effective teachers recognize that some students enter TK with skills that will enable them to progress to the next level far more rapidly than their peers. Differentiated instruction addresses the needs of proficient and advanced learners, as well as the needs of students who would benefit from additional support and more focused instruction. As evidence about students' current levels of performance is gathered from both formal and informal assessments, instruction is then tailored to meet the assessed needs of each student and promote his or her maximum growth.

Planning Differentiated Instruction

After teachers identify their students' current levels of performance, they then identify the "next-step" for each student. Highly skilled teachers "possess an extensive repertoire of skills and strategies they are able to draw upon, and they know how and when to choose among them, to effectively promote each child's learning and development at that moment" (Copple and Bredekamp 2009, 18). Teachers scaffold children's learning by providing appropriate support to achieve their next learning goal. Teachers then gradually reduce the amount of support provided as the student begins to demonstrate increasing mastery.

To scaffold instruction and to address the assessed learning needs in a TK classroom, teachers might (see figure 5 on next page):

- Supply the classroom with a variety of open-ended materials and manipulatives that support learning and engage all students in a variety of auditory, visual, verbal, and tactile activities. Effective teachers use opportunities provided by the engaging and stimulating environments they engineer to note evidence of growth and to identify possible areas of need for their students. TK teachers also seek opportunities to interact with the students to informally differentiate instruction by reinforcing or reviewing concepts that have been introduced.

- Use various formats of instruction (e.g., one-on-one support, small-group and large-group instruction) to match the assessed needs of

students. Large-group experiences provide teachers with opportunities to introduce concepts and to share experiences with children. Large-group settings also provide students "with opportunities to practice skills such as talking to a group, listening to their classmates, responding appropriately with questions or comments" (Copple and Bredekamp 2009, 39). TK students benefit from teacher-led, small-group instruction that provides focused individualized support for concept development, opportunities to receive more specific feedback, and additional practice. Proficient and advanced TK students also benefit from small-group instruction that provides them with opportunities to extend their learning. Individual adult–child interactions provide optimal opportunities for focused differentiation.

- Vary the content and complexity of lessons and related questioning strategies to reflect attention to individual developmental needs. Although our goal for each child is the cognitive and social–emotional growth necessary for success in traditional kindergarten, effective TK teachers recognize that the path to this goal varies greatly for each child. Teachers scaffold growth by adjusting lesson content and using a variety of differentiated questioning strategies to build deep conceptual understanding before moving forward. Teachers tailor lesson complexity, the degree of scaffolding, and questioning strategies to meet the immediate needs of their students. When students demonstrate confidence and competence at a given level, teachers gradually decrease the amount of scaffolding and gently increase rigor to nudge children forward on their developmental paths.

- Provide extended learning opportunities and exploration for students who are demonstrating mastery.

- Permit students to work at their comfortable pace, allowing extra time as needed to avoid unnecessary frustration and to build and maintain a sense of competence.

- Partner students of different abilities to facilitate positive peer relationships and encourage peer support.

- Design learning environments that promote exploration based on students' interest.

- Adapt materials to meet the needs of students' varied skills and abilities.

- If possible, provide spaces where students have limited visual and auditory stimuli.

Quiet spaces encourage students to monitor themselves and calm down when necessary.

Summary

Assessment information is essential to teachers as they plan instruction. Effective teachers use observations and other assessment information they have gathered to inform their daily planning and to chart a path for success in kindergarten. They carefully and intentionally consider the learning experiences they will provide for the group as a whole, for small groups, and for individual students. Materials, environments, or routines are adapted based on assessed needs.

Figure 5: Differentiated Instruction

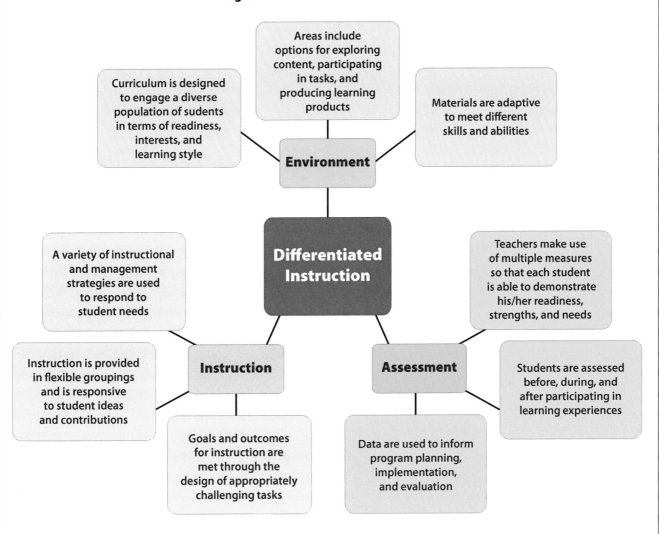

TK teachers use their understanding of child development and their knowledge of what each child needs to meet the goals of each student.

Communicating with Families About Student Learning

Families have a wealth of information to share about their children's interests, knowledge, skills, and dispositions toward learning. As the vignette below illustrates, a strong home–school partnership contributes to a well-rounded assessment of student abilities (Gullo 2006). In an effective TK program, teachers reach out to families to gather information. Teachers also provide ongoing information about their children's progress and welcome suggestions that can be easily incorporated into their daily activities to support their child's progress and enhance positive relationship. Teachers use a variety of means to include families in the assessment process. This section offers suggestions for both informal and formal opportunities for collaborative data collection, conversation, and reflection.

Informal Opportunities to Share Information

TK teachers have many informal opportunities to connect with families throughout the school year. Arrival and departure time, classroom visits, phone calls, and e-mails are common tools for sharing information (Kaczmarek 2007). Brief conversations

Vignette

Mr. Gonzalez conducts formal conferences with parents two or three times a year. He also recognizes the importance of ongoing informal communication about the children's progress. Each day, he informally observes three or four selected students for targeted skills as a part of his formative assessment process. He uses this information to inform his planning and to differentiate his instruction. He often records this information as evidence of student progress in formal assessment records as well. Earlier in the day, he noted that two of the students he wanted to observe were cooperating as they played with the tricycles. This is something they have been working on, and Mr. Gonzalez wants to share his observation with their parents. He takes a moment to jot a note to the parents in their home–school communication log, telling them how cooperative the children had been and thanking them for their continuing support.

Now, at the end of the day, Mr. Gonzalez stands at the door of his TK classroom saying good-bye to his students and families. As one student's family passes by, a parent stops to share a piece of paper and says in Spanish, "I am so proud of Olga. She drew this picture of her aunt at home. She even wrote 'Tia Liz' without much help." Mr. Gonzalez matches the parents' enthusiasm for their child's learning and asks in Spanish if he can make a copy of the writing sample to add to the student's portfolio. The parents smile and agree before patting their child on the shoulder. Mr. Gonzalez thanks the parents and encourages them to continue sharing important student work from home. He emphasizes the value of ongoing communication by saying, "Sharing this helps me to do my job as Olga's teacher at school!"

with individual families or communication through written correspondence can be used to highlight progress toward standards for learning. General information can also be shared with parents at parent orientation or Back-to-School Night. Explanations of the benefits of such home–school collaboration also reinforce this important partnership. Communication notebooks or journals sent home and returned to school promote the involvement of families who are not able to come to school. Bi-weekly or monthly newsletters can be used to address current group learning goals and offer additional ideas for at-home observation. For example, a teacher planning to explore counting and simple addition may invite families to engage their child in a similar experience at home. TK educators can then follow-up with individual progress at school and ask for details of learning from home.

Formal Opportunities to Share Information

Parent–teacher conferences are regularly scheduled meetings that provide opportunities for more in-depth conversations regarding a child's progress. "Effective parent–teacher conferences open the dialogue and offer a vehicle for establishing and strengthening partnerships with families" (Seplocha 2007, 12). During parent–teacher conferences, TK teachers share assessment data and work samples that illustrate each student's development.

Parents, are invited to share observations related to their child's individual progress at parent–teacher conferences. TK teachers may ask open-ended questions to help parents reflect on and describe the everyday learning that happens outside of school. This collective data will help inform both parties as they seek to generate future goals for learning and ideas for supporting student progress (Gullo 2006).

Suggestions for Formal Parent–Teacher Conferences

Formal conferences in TK programs provide an opportunity to lay a strong foundation for future parent–teacher/school partnerships. It is important to recognize that for many parents, these TK conferences are the first formal interactions they will have with an elementary school. To help ensure a positive experience for all, consider including the following with your appropriately translated invitations to attend the conference:

1. A brief outline of what will happen during the conference.

2. A reminder that families are invited to share information about the child, such as:

   • the child's favorite activities at home;

   • how the child likes to help at home;

   • other siblings and their ages;

   • the child's usual bedtime;

   • comments the child makes about his or her TK experience.

3. A reminder to come prepared with any questions they might have.

Summary

TK teachers who routinely make it a priority to invite parents to share information about their student's progress and to communicate with families about their students' development, strengthen home–school relationships and promote quality learning experiences for all students. A combination of informal conversation and the sharing of work samples, paired with formal parent–teacher conferences offer multiple opportunities for communication. Additional ideas for involving families in TK classrooms to enhance program quality and instruction are discussed in chapter 7.

CHAPTER 7
Involving Families and Community Partners in a Transitional Kindergarten Program

Involving Families and Community Partners in a Transitional Kindergarten Program
http://www4.scoe.net/ims/webcasts/cf/index.
cfm?fuseaction=archivedDetail&eventID=140&archiveID=256

Involving Families and Community Partners in a Transitional Kindergarten Program
(YouTube with Captions)
http://www.youtube.com/watch?v=w8SEQpJVVs0watch?v=w8SEQpJVVs0

Relationships are at the core of all groups and community dynamics. Research tells us that who we are, the people we spend time with, and the settings in which we live all shape our lives. A child's development is influenced and shaped by ongoing, and often simultaneous, interactions and relationships with family, friends, and neighbors in school, church and the community (McDevitt and Ormrod 2004). Being mindful of external influences on learning and development is important as TK teachers seek to educate students and engage families in the school system. Research has also found a significant relationship between the home–school partnership and student achievement (Esptein and Sheldon 2006; Henderson and Mapp 2002; Jeynes 2005). Schools that make efforts to create partnerships with community organizations and public stakeholders promote the school's impact in the neighborhood and connect families with community programs. Attending to these overlapping spheres of influence can have a positive influence on academic outcomes (Epstein 2001). In this chapter, methods for establishing interconnected and interdependent relationships with families and communities are reviewed. Special attention is given to recognizing, understanding, and honoring the diverse settings and experiences of families, neighborhoods and communities. For the purposes of the TK Implementation Guide, the terms "family" and "parent" are used interchangeably to refer to the significant primary caregivers in a child's life as described in chapter 5.

Communicating About Transitional Kindergarten with Family and Community Partners

TK programs offer children and families engaging learning environments that are designed to meet the social–emotional and cognitive needs of young students. Many families and community members may not be familiar with the purpose and structure of the TK program. School administrators and teachers can schedule events to introduce the district model for TK instruction to parents, school partners, and community-based organizations. Information regarding the purpose and intent of the TK program and how young students will benefit from participating in the program should be highlighted at these events.

Vignette

Wenqi's mother and grandfather sit at the family dinner table speaking in Mandarin about the recent TK orientation they attended. "I think we should go to the TK Family Night. It will be a nice way for Wenqi to meet some of her classmates and for us to meet other families," says Wenqi's mother, "And it is at our local community center, next to the children's library." They shift the conversation to discuss the different ways Mr. Gee encourages family involvement in his TK classroom. "I don't feel comfortable speaking in English," says Wenqi's grandfather, "and isn't it a teacher's job to plan school lessons? Why are they asking for parents to be in the classroom? I want Wenqi to know that Mr. Gee is her teacher. Won't it confuse her to have so many adults in the classroom?" "I understand," replies Wenqi's mother, "but I believe Mr. Gee is making an effort to learn about the different families of his students. I also like when he said that a parent is a child's first teacher. I think we could help Wenqi feel comfortable in her new school if we shared some of our home culture with the rest of the students. I don't want Wenqi to forget her family roots." They continue the conversation, sharing their different views and perspectives as they discuss additional options for participating in the TK program.

Community events, such as TK parent presentations or TK Information Nights, can be used to educate families and address the purpose of TK programs. Parents benefit from opportunities to meet other parents and stakeholders and by being able to raise questions, express their views and concerns, and contribute ideas related to the TK program. (School staff members should use written communication in home languages to communicate with families when appropriate). The use of newsletters, class Web sites, and brochures heighten awareness and knowledge of TK instruction. Community partners, including family health workers, and public and private preschools, can also assist with providing information about TK programs.

Engaging Families in the Transitional Kindergarten Classroom

Research affirms the importance of family engagement in early education (Weissbourd, Weissbourd, and O'Carroll 2010). Parent involvement in school settings has been associated with the following student outcomes (Henderson and Mapp 2002, 24):

- Higher academic achievement, as indicated by grade point averages and scores on standardized tests or rating scales

- Enrollment in more challenging academic programs

- More classes passed and credits earned

- Better attendance at school

- Improved behavior at home and at school

- Better social skills and adjustment to school

School administrators and teachers set the tone for family involvement. An important factor in creating effective partnerships is creating a climate of trust where school staff and parents see themselves as valued and equal partners in the educational process.

Preparing Teachers to Partner with Families

Educators impact student achievement by directly influencing the development of students, but they also have the opportunity to promote positive relationships with parents. The relationships that TK teachers establish with families shape parent involvement and impact student learning outcomes. Research findings indicate that the degree to which parents are involved in their child's education is correlated with school achievement. Students of highly involved parents score substantially higher on academic measures than peers with less involved parents (Jeynes 2005).

Building authentic partnerships begins with staff development that focuses on working with families. The intent is to "find significant points of entry into parents' lives" (Weissbourd, Weissbourd, and O'Carroll 2010, 115) and to promote meaningful family engagement. As mentioned in chapter 8, staff development on family engagement should not be limited to one session. Instead, school administrators and teachers need to revisit concepts over time and in a variety of contexts (e.g., workshops, peer mentoring, and informal conversations).

For TK teachers, building relationships with parents at the beginning of the school year is an important area of focus. Educators and parents "need time to get to know one another, plan how they will work together to increase student learning, and carry out their plan" (Funkhouser and Gonzales 1997, 11). Regular contact throughout the academic year sustains quality relationships and further encourages parent engagement. After initial connections have been made, teachers can plan and prepare opportunities for family involvement in and out of the TK classroom. School events, such as parent orientation and Back to School Night, are ideal settings for parents and teachers to get to know one another and share their ideas for family engagement. Informal gatherings can also be used to plan and implement school partnerships. Educators increase family involvement when they take into consideration parent ideas, interests, and needs (Henderson and Mapp 2002). TK teachers can provide families with information and training about how to participate in partnerships. Specific strategies for partnering with families are listed in the Resource Box below.

Some TK programs may not be able to implement all of these methods for relationship building, as the families' proximity to school, time constraints, and work schedules may limit their options. TK

teachers can select the methods that best fit the needs of their programs. Ongoing involvement with parents—such as casual conversations at arrival and drop-off times, sharing anecdotes from school, asking about home experiences, and

Ideas for Family Involvement

The following is an introductory list for encouraging parent participation in the TK classroom. Additional ideas for family involvement can be generated by teachers to reflect individual family strengths, interests, resources, and schedules.

On-site/classroom opportunities:

- Share a hobby, talent, or occupation
- Read stories to individual children or in small groups
- Attend field trips
- Facilitate classroom activities
- Share a cultural tradition

Off-site/at-home opportunities:

- Create homemade curriculum supplies
- Read and record stories or music
- Donate real objects and recyclables
- Make name badges for school outings

School staff members can also encourage parent support of school activities by providing workshops and resources for extending learning into the home. Lessons embedded in family experiences, such as shopping for groceries, are more easily incorporated into home routines. Lending libraries and take-home activities may also be sent home to invite further learning and discovery.

planning opportunities for parents to contribute to the classroom—is an effective approach to further these significant networks. Extra effort can be made to strengthen relationships with family members who may not be able to be present at school on a regular basis. Teachers can also strengthen family connections through phone conversations, e-mails, or written correspondence with parents.

Diverse Backgrounds and Experiences of Families

Diversity includes "the myriad experiences and attributes that contribute to each person's uniqueness, regardless of cultural or ethnic heritage or community, such as social class, gender, occupational status, income, sexual orientation, ability, disability, religion, and education" (Adelabu, Durand, and Jenkins-Scott 2010, 15–16). This inclusive definition makes it clear that each student and family enters the TK classroom with a unique background and personal history. How teachers and other educators view and respond to this diversity has an important influence on student learning and family engagement. Educators can communicate their value and respect for family identity as they welcome students and their families into the TK learning community. As TK teachers seek to create and engage family support in the classroom, time can be spent learning about each family's strengths and interests. By recognizing that all families have unique talents, skills, and life experiences, teachers communicate the importance and necessity of the role of parents in the education of children. There are many ways to initiate positive relationships with families—for example, through home visits and socialization opportunities at school. Informal meetings open the conversation for learning about individual family strengths and resources.

TK teachers and other school staff members need to keep in mind that families come to school with expectations for their children. While all families

"want their children to be successful in school, complexities of culture, family background, language, values, and attitudes frame and influence the way families view education and their role in supporting it" (Adelabu, Durand, and Jenkins-Scott 2010, 15). It is important that school professionals work together to make schools personal and welcoming to families. Programs can empower parents and help them define the "parent role" as being an active member of the educational team (Henderson and Mapp 2002). TK teachers support parents when they draw attention to the important skills and knowledge that families share with their children. Chapter 4 provides additional information about the important role that effective teacher–parent engagement plays in instructional planning.

Engagement of Community Partners

Establishing connections with local businesses, health care providers, and other community service agencies enriches TK programs and instruction. While familiarity and respect are integral to family involvement, they are also necessary for engaging public partners. School administrators and teachers who spend time in the surrounding community become aware of its history and of current interests, needs, and resources (York 2003). They can extend student learning by going out into the community and inviting community members to the school to share their expertise. For example, TK teachers can take students on a field trip to a local business or invite a dentist to visit the classroom to speak about oral health. Community organizations have much to offer students and families outside of the school day. School staff members who are knowledgeable about community-based organizations can connect families with programs that support reading, writing, and other areas of learning during evening hours, on weekends, and in the summer months (Henderson and Mapp 2002). Family resource centers can support families in need of health care, mental health services, or vocational services. Schools can also seek partnerships with community service groups to improve school facilities, outdoor play spaces, and community centers. Community stakeholders involved with the school's commitment to learning and vision for community engagement can become enthusiastic and willing partners in meeting student and family needs.

Summary

Schools that build authentic partnerships with families "view student achievement as a shared responsibility, and all stakeholders—including parents, administrators, teachers, and community leaders—play important roles in supporting children's learning" (Funkhouser and Gonzales 1997, 3). Research confirms the immediate and long-term benefits of family and community involvement on student success. Time invested in professional development, relationship building, and ongoing partnerships leaves a lasting impact on children, families, and communities.

CHAPTER 8
Supporting Transitional Kindergarten Implementation

Supporting Transitional Kindergarten Implementation
http://www4.scoe.net/ims/webcasts/cf/index.
cfm?fuseaction=archivedDetail&eventID=140&archiveID=257

Supporting Transitional Kindergarten Implementation (YouTube with Captions)
http://www.youtube.com/watch?v=4HaAwQa7Q_A

This chapter is organized into three separate but related sections: (1) Teacher Qualifications and Early Education Experiences, (2) Staffing Patterns to Support Transitional Kindergarten Students, and (3) Professional Learning.

Teacher Qualifications and Early Education Experiences

As school and district administrators prepare to enroll students in TK classrooms, they recruit and employ teachers who have the required credentials. However, administrators should also consider each teacher's experience in working with young children. Procedures to ensure that teachers are assigned to TK classes based on their qualifications and appropriateness will be important considerations for school districts. This section covers criteria for selecting TK teaching staff, including critical areas of educational and professional knowledge.

Foundations in Child Development

Although credential requirements are addressed in chapter 1, possession of a valid teaching credential does not ensure that a candidate has the knowledge and experience related to child development. A teacher who understands standards for learning and who also possesses knowledge of child development is well equipped to promote student school success (Siraj-Blatchford et al. 2002). Knowing what students should learn and how children grow supports teachers as they prepare quality learning environments, nurture relationships, and plan appropriately challenging academic lessons and activities. It is also important that educators stay current with new research and findings related to development and early education. As an example, recent research highlights the importance of engaging children in activities that prompt representational thought (Ritchie, Maxwell, and Bredekamp 2009), such as asking children to draw or act out what they know.

Vignette

It is morning meeting time in Ms. Spier's TK classroom. Principal Barahona observes as Ms. Spier leads her students through the greeting song, calendar, and attendance activity. It is only the second week of school but the students are already actively participating in the simple welcome routines. Ms. Spier begins a short lesson on the classroom rules. She first reminds the students of the rules they were introduced to during their first week of school: Be Safe, Be Respectful, Be Friendly. "Today," she says, "I want to talk more about being safe. I am going to hand each of you a 'green light' and a 'red light' sign. Gabrielle and Yoon-Seo, can you pass one of each color to your friends? Thank you for your help. Now, I am going to tell you about a behavior, and you show me whether it is a STOP (holds up the red light) or a GO (holds up the green light) behavior. Ready?" She holds up a picture of running feet and says, "Is it a stop? Or a go?" The children hold up their red lights and reply, "STOP!" The teacher replies, "That's right! It's a stop. Where is it okay to run?" "Outside!" say the children. As Ms. Spier continues to discuss ways to meet the expectation of being safe at school, Principal Barahona smiles to herself. She is pleased to have selected Ms. Spier for her new TK program. She recalls how impressed she was with Ms. Spier's initial interview for the position. She shared examples of her work in early education and discussed the importance of supporting social–emotional development in the TK year. With such a strong effort by Ms. Spier to front-load expectations for student participation and learning, Principal Barahona is confident it will be a great year in Ms. Spier's TK classroom.

Teachers who use this interactive instructional and assessment approach are better able to assess knowledge, shape understanding, and promote conceptual development. Research points to the importance of student-initiated independent exploration in early education. While direct instruction is useful for providing introductory information and offering explanations, it must be paired with active learning experiences to ensure depth of understanding.

Effective educators view their work as a professional journey where they evolve and grow over time. They are passionate, they persevere through challenges, they are willing to take risks, and they are patient (Colker 2008). Skilled educators also show flexibility in their work, adapting to new challenges with high energy and creativity. As shared in *Becoming a Critically Reflective Teacher*, "one of the hardest things teachers have to learn is that the sincerity of their intentions does not guarantee the purity of their practice" (Brookfield 1995, 1). Effective teachers use self-reflection as a tool for evaluating their personal strengths and the areas that are in need of improvement. Many teachers enter their first year of TK instruction with the knowledge base,

skills, and attitudes necessary for effective teaching and high levels of learning for children. However, ongoing professional development will increase their ability to be effective teachers. Professional development and partnerships can do much to enhance and extend teacher competencies.

Staffing Patterns to Support Transitional Kindergarten Students

To meet the needs of all TK students, administrators and teachers can work together to build and maintain collaborative partnerships with each other as well as with program assistants. Classroom assistance can be provided by teaching teams and/or other adult support for the classroom. Funding will determine the ability to employ paraeducators and school assistants, but programs can also enlist parent and community volunteers to assist in classrooms. Districts can consider a variety of funding streams to support TK classrooms. As discussed in chapter 1, funding sources such as Title I, Title II, or Title III funds, as well as possible new early learning funds, are potential resources to support professional development or to

Vignette

Mr. Lopez, the morning TK teacher, and Miss Holmes, the afternoon TK teacher, meet during their weekly in-service time to discuss student progress, reflect on their recent classroom experiences, and share their upcoming lesson plans. Mr. Lopez highlights the positive learning outcomes he observed during English language arts instruction, and he says, "I am feeling a bit frustrated by the geometry activity we had implemented. The students seemed to struggle with describing the characteristics of flat shapes. Did you observe that with your group?" "Yes, I noticed that too," replies Miss Holmes. "It seems that we may need to spend a bit more time defining the shape traits. I wonder if we need more concrete objects for them to hold and manipulate," "How about if we give the children different examples of the same shape—real manipulatives—to help them generalize the defining attributes? We can sing a shape song to engage them in music and movement," says Mr. Lopez. "The song cues the children to hold up shapes as they are shouted in the lyrics. This will give us a chance to check for individual and group understanding," adds Miss Holmes. The two teachers continue the conversation to assign tasks for environment and activity preparation in their shared space.

expand staffing support for TK. In this section, the importance of establishing collaborative partnerships focused on shared vision and mutual respect is discussed along with ideas for enlisting and using support staff.

Collaborative Partnerships

Children learn in the context of relationships, and the same is true for adults. As noted by Biddle (2012), observing colleagues in action and conversing about differences in practice can inspire new ideas, promote reflection, and further enhance program quality. Wherever possible, administrators can support TK programs to work in collaboration with each other. These educational partnerships are more easily generated and sustained when TK teachers are available to each other. Overlapping teaching schedules, classrooms located in close proximity, or shared room assignments invite close, collaborative relationships among educators. Teachers and other school staff who work in single programs or those who are long distances from other programs can be provided opportunities to work with other TK professionals. Administrators can play an important role in facilitating these distant connections by designating time, fostering professional networks, and encouraging varied forms of professional partnership. Examples, such as online professional development communities, visual media, and distance learning are valuable forms of administrative support.

Once collaborative relationships are established, teachers can work together to create shared goals for program planning, implementation, and evaluation. Teamwork may be employed in the creation, staging, and maintenance of the learning environment. These working relationships can be used to enhance instruction as educators engage in reflective practice (see the highlight on the following page). The foundation of all effective working relationships is open communication. Attention can be focused on the use of active listening, considering another person's point of view, opinion, and experience.

Enlisting Support Staff

As discussed in chapter 4, adult–child relationships have an important impact on student learning and academic success. Decreasing the adult-to-child ratio in TK classrooms increases the opportunities for students to make meaningful connections with teachers and staff, and it promotes the implementation of differentiated instruction. Administrators can staff TK classrooms with paraeducators or teaching aides if the school and program budgets can cover the costs. Additional staffing is especially important at the beginning of the school year when TK students need extra support as they transition and adapt to school rules and routines. Where funding is limited, extra program support can be sought from parents, family members, and community volunteers. Recruiting and sustaining a volunteer TK workforce can be accomplished by communicating the value of program assistance and offering a variety of ways to help, such as leading small-group activities or creating homemade curriculum supplies at home. TK teachers may choose to involve volunteer assistants throughout the daily routine and in curriculum activities. To assist the support staff in effectively carrying out program plans, teachers can share details about their philosophy of education and their goals for student learning. This will provide a framework for program practice and instruction. TK teachers can ensure that classroom assistants meet the necessary standards for learning by providing, in advance of the lesson, clear instructions and ideas for engaging diverse learners.

Educators who work with team members and support staff build collegial partnerships. Curriculum is generated through collaborative planning, implementation, and reflection by TK teachers. Professional and volunteer staff members help in the preparation of curriculum materials and assist with instruction. Programs can find ways to recruit and maintain parents, family members, or community volunteers to support student learning.

Reflective Practice within Collaborative Partnerships

Although it is important for teachers to spend time alone to reflect on their professional process, it is also valuable for them to engage in reflection with colleagues (Biddle 2012). Reflective practice is an interactive dialogue in which individuals discuss educational beliefs, instructional practices, professional progress, and achievements. To support this type of professional development, teachers and administrators should prioritize time for reflective meetings. The frequency of these meetings will vary, depending on the program design (full-day versus half-day programs), teaching schedules, proximity of support, and integration of technology (e.g., online discussion forums). The following questions (Crane 2007) may be used in reflective practice:

- What are your goals? What are you trying to accomplish?
- What have you tried so far?
- How have your efforts worked (or not worked)? What results have you achieved so far?
- What kinds of problems have you encountered? What solutions have you tried?
- What do you see as other options?
- What is your plan for moving forward?

The reflective process may be enhanced and made more concrete through the use of several tools:

- Videotaping: Ask a colleague to videotape a large-group lesson or set up a tripod in the classroom to capture interactions with students.
- Photos: Use a digital camera to document students engaged in various activities throughout the day.
- Written records: Keep small clipboards with paper and pencils in various spots in the classroom to record student questions and comments.
- Journaling: Take a few moments at the end of the day to pause and write down observations of student work or personal reflections about a small-group activity.
- Assessment data: Review written records and evidence from student portfolios to assess development and student progress over time.

Professional Learning

Research on professional development has long been associated with positive outcomes in classroom instruction and student learning (National Research Council 2001; Yoon et al. 2007). Data also emphasize the importance of pairing professional learning opportunities with follow-up support (Pianta 2011). To be effective,

Vignette

Ms. Chang creates her lesson plan from the recent TK Institute she attended. As she browses through the handouts and resources she collected, her excitement for the upcoming school year grows. She is eager to share with her school administrator the topics covered during the two-day event. Ms. Chang especially enjoyed the sessions related to classroom management and assessment; these topics will help round out her professional work as she transitions from first grade to TK. Ms. Chang also wants to seek her administrator's support for joining a regional and district professional learning community. At the institute, she met several teachers, specialists, and administrators who intend to form a cohort designed to support and enhance current knowledge, personal attitudes, and professional development for regional and district TK staff. Ms. Chang is certain that her participation in the cohort will help her apply the concepts learned at the institute and assist with the planning, implementation, and evaluation of her TK program.

professional development experiences must be "aligned, systematic, [and] sequenced" (Albrecht and Engel 2007, 18). The following section provides recommendations for formal and informal professional development, as well as topics for enhancing TK teacher instruction and classroom management.

Professional development is an important way to support teachers who are in the midst of planning and implementing TK programs. District and school administrators who regularly plan professional development opportunities offer educators different access points for training that can be tailored to meet the individual needs of the teaching staff. Formal opportunities for professional development include in-service workshops, institutes, conferences, professional learning communities, and classes offered by school sites, district, county office of education, or other agencies. Formal sessions yield the best results when they are conducted over time and include ongoing support for learning (The Education Alliance 2008). While administrators and the public may seek immediate change in schools and student outcomes, teachers need time to make change. Teachers need sufficient opportunities to prepare, implement, and evaluate new strategies for program design and instruction. Implementation of these new strategies will be enhanced with the assistance of a team teacher, mentor, and or professional development coach.

There are many ways for teachers to expand their knowledge of child development, instruction, and active learning experiences for TK students. Opportunities for articulation with other TK teachers at a school site or within a district provide teachers with possibilities for collegial connections and opportunities for collaborative program planning. Educators can work together as they apply information shared at formal professional development sessions. TK teachers have much to gain from extending their working relationships to include preschool, kindergarten, and first-grade teachers. Through articulation, teachers are better able to generate shared educational goals and methods for reaching individual and group

Professional Learning Communities and Transitional Kindergarten

Professional learning communities were developed in the mid-1990s to increase professional knowledge and improve student outcomes. To apply current research and best practices in education, teachers and administrators involved in professional learning communities "continuously seek and share learning and then act on what they learn" (Southwest Educational Development Laboratory 1997). According to the Center for Comprehensive School Reform and Improvement (2009), common characteristics of these learning communities include:

- shared values and vision;
- a collaborative culture;
- a focus on examining outcomes to improve student learning;
- supportive and shared leadership;
- shared personal practice.

Teachers and administrators benefit from participating in professional learning communities that are focused specifically on TK development, implementation, and evaluation. These learning communities are a source of support and encouragement as professionals seek to develop effective TK programs.

learning goals. A holistic view of child development in early education is created through collective dialogue and expertise. Visiting varied early education programs and observing in classrooms as students engage with materials and attend to instruction can also further expand teacher knowledge. Teachers who regularly engage in such formal and informal meetings with other educational staff support the refinement of instructional practices and pace academic learning appropriately by staying informed of curricular goals and approaches over time.

All educators benefit from coaching and supervision that is encouraging and validating, as well as constructive in terms of feedback. Open-ended questions allow teachers to share their knowledge and perspectives and can provide background information about teacher instruction. Additionally, mentors and supervisors who are sensitive to teachers' ideas and concerns invite dialogue about future plans for professional development (Albrecht and Engel 2007). In addition to partnering with other school professionals, TK teachers can work independently to improve their professional work. Journaling offers a judgment-free medium for exploring personal beliefs and practices in education. Teachers can also use journals to document their professional journeys, revisiting experiences, themes, and ideas for instruction over time. Web sites can also offer rich resources for environment planning, curriculum, and instruction. Some caution needs to be taken in utilizing online tools; the credibility of the source should be researched prior to acceptance and use.

Professional Development Topics

Administrators should enlist teachers as active participants in the selection of topics for professional development (The Education Alliance 2008). Educators who are asked to identify what they want to learn are more engaged, motivated, and committed to the professional development process. TK teachers may be concerned with supplementing their educational and professional expertise to work with TK students. For example, they may want information about what to expect in the first day, first week, and first month of the TK year. Other general topics that are important for TK professional development include social–emotional development of the TK student, classroom management, assessment, partnering with parents, and oral language as a focal point for instruction. Below are several important resources for TK program planning and instruction:

- *The Alignment of the California Preschool Learning Foundations with Key Early Education Resources*: *California Infant/Toddler Learning and Development Foundations, California Content Standards, the Common Core State Standards, and Head Start Child Development and Early Learning Framework*

- Content Standards for California Public Schools

- California's Common Core State Standards for English Language Arts and Mathematics

- California Preschool Learning Foundations

- California Preschool Curriculum Framework

Summary

Professional development is necessary for program, teacher, and student success in any educational setting. Administrators and teachers can be kept up-to-date and informed about educational research, strategies for instruction, and methods of classroom management. Formal and informal professional development can serve complementary purposes in teacher education. Formal professional development is most effective when paired with informal opportunities to revisit, implement, and refine new concepts in instruction and classroom management. As teachers embark on their professional journeys, administrators effectively engage them in the professional development process by inviting them to share ideas for action and topics for consideration.

GLOSSARY

accommodations. Changes made to the curriculum or instruction that enhance a student's access to the learning setting but do not change the overall expectations of the activity.

active learning. A dynamic approach to education that engages students in direct and immediate curricular experiences with objects, people, ideas, and events and cultivates their understanding through discussion and reflection. An emphasis is placed on responding to individual and group initiative and attending to student motivation, inquiry, and problem solving.

adaptations. Modifications and accommodations made to the curriculum, teaching methodology, classroom learning environment, and materials to increase access to learning opportunities and educational success.

articulation. The systematic coordination of course and/or program content within and between educational institutions and agencies to facilitate effective advancement in student learning from grade to grade, school to school, and from school to the working world.

assistive technology. An item or equipment used to maintain or improve the participation of a student with a disability in an inclusive setting. Assistive technology can be used to support implementation of universal design for learning.

conceptual learning. A process by which students learn how to organize information based on well-sequenced learning experiences that reference previously learned material, introduce new skills and knowledge, and join concepts together, applying them to real-world situations. Conceptual learning curriculum promotes inquiry and curiosity so that students want to understand the material and are driven to learn more.

Desired Results Developmental Profile–School Readiness (DRDP-SR©). A valid, reliable measurement tool for observing, documenting, and reflecting on the learning, development, and progress of transitional kindergarten students and traditional kindergarten students. The DRDP-SR is aligned with the California Preschool Learning Foundations, the California Kindergarten Content Standards, and the Common Core State Standards.

differentiated assessment. The process of selecting a range of tools and strategies to provide each student with the best opportunity to demonstrate his or her readiness, strengths, and needs in relation to specific outcomes and activities.

differentiated instruction. The framework or philosophy for effective teaching that involves modifying and adapting instruction, materials, content, student projects and products, and assessment so that all students within a classroom can learn effectively.

emotional regulation. A person's ability to understand his or her emotional experience and respond with an appropriate range of immediate and delayed emotions.

family resource center. A community-based location that provides services for families such as health, mental health, and education.

flexible grouping. Variable use of group size (e.g., large- and small-group, partner, and individual work), membership (e.g., heterogeneous or homogeneous), and/or materials to differentiate instruction within a community of learners.

front-loading. Using activities to prepare students for what is to come and teach them skills and strategies to be applied in future educational and social contexts.

horizontal articulation. The scope and integration of curriculum across all knowledge domains of the same course at the same level.

IEP. Abbreviation for "individualized education program." Written during a meeting attended by special and general educators, specialists, and parents, the purpose of an IEP is to identify special education supports and services for qualified children, ages three through twenty-one.

inclusion. According to the DEC/NAEYC (2009), "Early childhood inclusion embodies the values, policies, and practices that support the right of every infant and young child and his or her family, regardless of ability, to participate in a broad range of activities and context as full members of families, communities, and society. The desired results of inclusive experiences for children with and without disabilities and their families include a sense of belonging and membership, positive social relationships and friendships, and development and learning to reach their full potential. The defining features of inclusion that can be used to identify high quality early childhood programs and services are access, participation, and supports."

inclusive practice. The process of creating an acceptance of differences within the general education classroom by adapting methodologies, curriculum, and environments so that all children can experience a sense of belonging, access, and participation with typically developing peers of the same age group.

integrated instruction. A teaching strategy that brings together curriculum and academic standards from more than one content area so that students explore and understand topics deeply.

intentional teaching. Acting with knowledge of specific development and educational

outcomes, and instructing with the purpose of challenging students, scaffolding, and extending learning so that students acquire the knowledge and skills they need to succeed in school and life.

journaling. A professional development tool for educators to promote reflective practice in classroom planning and instruction. Teachers regularly record and review classroom experiences to develop an awareness and understanding of their educational practices and to improve as instructors.

modalities. The different styles used by learners to concentrate on, process, and retain information. Learners may gather information visually, aurally, tactually, or by using combinations of these three methods.

modifications. Changes to the curriculum or teaching strategy that substantially alter the overall standards of expected performance in order for a student to achieve success.

multiple measures. The use of multiple indicators, assessment tools, and other sources of evidence of student learning, gathered at multiple points in time, to identify the strengths and needs of students so that curriculum may be adapted to meet individual knowledge and abilities.

professional learning communities. Environments in which teachers and administrators interact and collaborate regularly around issues of teaching and learning to seek and develop improved practices and processes for student learning.

purposeful play. Intrinsically motivated play in which students gather and process information, learn new skills, and practice old ones. Purposeful play is enhanced by the intentional scaffolding of teachers and the deliberate placement of challenging tools, materials, and resources.

running commentary. Narrating one's actions or the actions of another out loud for the purposes of supporting language acquisition, conceptual understanding, and problem solving.

scaffolding. A process by which adults or capable peers provide supportive structures to help students learn. Scaffolding is useful when students are confronted with a challenge that they can solve with a simple hint, question, model, or prompt.

self-efficacy. Measure of one's own ability to perform specific tasks and reach goals.

self-regulation. The complex cognitive process that allows individuals to alter their behavior to meet internal or social standards, ideals, or goals.

social dispositions. Innate character traits, both positive (e.g., cooperative, curious, inventive) and negative (e.g., closed-minded, selfish, argumentative), that are supported or weakened by interactive experiences in an environment with significant adults and peers.

social–emotional competence. Refers to the social, emotional, and cognitive skills and behaviors needed to succeed as a member of society. The expected skills and behaviors required for healthy social development vary by age and sociocultural context.

social knowledge and understanding. The ability to recognize, comprehend, and apply the behavioral expectations of a particular group, organization, or community.

social skills. The range of appropriate strategies used in interacting and communicating with others.

special education. A free and appropriate public education in the least restrictive environment for students who are eligible for services under the Individuals with Disabilities Education Act (IDEA) of 2004. The law requires the development of an IEP to determine the type and amount of specialized services, aids, and supports needed for a student to be successful in an educational program.

specially designed instruction. As defined by Title 34, Section 300.39(b)(3) of the *Code of Federal Regulations*, "*specially designed instruction* means adapting, as appropriate to the needs of an eligible child under this part, the content, methodology, or delivery of instruction to address the unique needs of the child that result from the child's disability; and to ensure access of the child to the general curriculum, so that the child can meet the educational standards within the jurisdiction of the public agency that apply to all children."[†]

student-initiated work experiences. Activities that proceed primarily along the lines of student interests and actions, with the teacher acting as a facilitator of learning who uses questions, prompts, and commentary to extend knowledge.

teacher-initiated work experiences. Activities that proceed primarily along the lines of the teacher's goals to introduce information and demonstrate skills. However, these experiences are also shaped by student interests and active engagement.

vertical articulation. Linkage of curriculum from level to level and within and across institutions that is intended to promote continuity of learning experiences.

wait time. The length of time an educator waits for student response after asking a question. Longer wait time affords students the opportunity to think and conceptualize a response and is associated with an increase in the length and quality of student answers.

[†]Refer to the Electronic Code of Federal Regulations (e-CFR) for more information.

REFERENCES

Adelabu, D., T. Durand, and J. Jenkins-Scott. 2010. "Full-Service Community Schools." In *Children of 2020: Creating a Better Tomorrow*, edited by V. Washington and J. Andrews,13–18. Washington, DC: Council for Professional Recognition.

Albrecht, K., and B. Engel. 2007. "Viewpoint: Moving Away from a Quick-Fix Mentality to Systematic Professional Development." *Young Children* 62:18–25.

Averill, O. H., and C. Rinaldi. 2011. "Research Brief: Multi-tier System of Supports (MTSS)." Waltham, MA: Urban Special Education Leadership Collaborative. https://www.urbancollaborative.org/sites/urbancollaborative.org/files/mtss_brief_final.modified_1.pdf (accessed July 29, 2013).

Bakley, S. 2001. "Through the Lens of Sensory Integration: A Different Way of Analyzing Challenging Behavior." *Young Children* 56:70–76.

Bennett, T. 2007. "Mapping Family Resources and Support." In *Spotlight on Young Children and Families*, edited by D. Koralek, 20–23. Washington, DC: National Association for the Education of Young Children.

Biddle, J. K. 2012. *The Three Rs of Leadership: Building Effective Early Childhood Programs Through Relationships, Reciprocal Learning, and Reflection.* Ypsilanti, MI: HighScope Press.

Brookfield, S. D. 1995. *Becoming a Critically Reflective Teacher.* San Francisco: Jossey-Bass.

California Commission on Teacher Credentialing. 2011. "Credential Information Alert: Transitional Kindergarten Assignments." http://www.siacabinetreport.com/admin/uploads/articleresources/8312011825536943.pdf (accessed July 29, 2013).

California County Superintendents Educational Services Association (CCSESA). 2011. *Transitional Kindergarten (TK) Planning Guide: A Resource for Administrators of California Public School Districts.* Sacramento, CA: Sacramento County Office of Education.

California Department of Education (CDE). 1999. *First Class: A Guide for Early Primary Education, Preschool–Kindergarten–First Grade.* Sacramento, CA: CDE.

———. 2000. *Prekindergarten Learning and Development Guidelines.* Sacramento, CA: CDE.

———. 2008. *California Preschool Learning Foundations, Volume 1.* Sacramento, CA: CDE.

———. 2009a. *California Infant/Toddler Learning and Development Foundations.* Sacramento, CA: CDE.

———. 2009b. *Preschool English Learners: Principles and Practices to Promote Language, Literacy, and Learning.* 2nd ed. Sacramento, CA: CDE.

———. 2010a. *California Preschool Curriculum Framework, Volume 1.* Sacramento, CA: CDE.

———. 2010b. *California Preschool Learning Foundations, Volume 2.* Sacramento, CA: CDE.

———. 2011. *California Preschool Curriculum Framework, Volume 2.* Sacramento, CA: CDE.

———. 2012a. Desired Results Developmental Profile–School Readiness (DRDP-SR©). http://drdpsr.org (accessed July 29, 2013).

———. 2012b. *English Language Development Standards for California Public Schools, Kindergarten Through Grade Twelve.* http://www.cde.ca.gov/sp/el/er/eldstandards.asp (accessed July 29, 2013).

———. 2012c. *The Alignment of the California Preschool Learning Foundations with Key Early Education Resources: California Infant/Toddler Learning and Development Foundations, California Content Standards, Common Core State Standards, and Head Start Child Development and*

Early Learning Framework. Sacramento, CA: CDE. http://www.cde.ca.gov/sp/cd/re/documents/psalignment.pdf (accessed July 29, 2013).

———. 2012d. Title III—Immigrant Program Overview. http://www.cde.ca.gov/sp/el/t3/immprogrview.asp (accessed July 29, 2013).

———. 2013a. *California Preschool Curriculum Framework, Volume 3.* Sacramento, CA: CDE.

———. 2013b. *California Preschool Learning Foundations, Volume 3.* Sacramento, CA: CDE.

———. 2013c. Language Census: English Learner Students by Language by Grade. http://dq.cde.ca.gov/dataquest/ (accessed June 12, 2013).

———. 2013d. Title 1, Part A, CalEd facts. http://www.cde.ca.gov/sp/sw/t1/ceft1pa.asp (accessed July 29, 2013).

———. 2013e. California Laws & Codes. Data file. http://www.cde.ca.gov/re/lr/cl (accessed July 29, 2013).

California Senate Bill No. 1381. 2010. Chapter 705, Legislative Council's Digest. http://www.leginfo.ca.gov/pub/09-10/bill/sen/sb_1351-1400/sb_1381_bill_20100930_chaptered.pdf (accessed July 30, 2013).

Cannon, J. S., and S. Lipscomb. 2008. *Changing the Kindergarten Cutoff Date: Effects on California Students and Schools.* San Francisco: Public Policy Institute of California. http://www.ppic.org/main/publication.asp?i=825 (accessed July 29, 2013).

Center for Applied Special Technology (CAST). 1999. Universal Design for Learning. http://www.cast.org/research/udl/ (accessed July 29, 2013).

The Center for Comprehensive School Reform and Improvement. 2009. Professional Learning Communities. http://www.centerforcsri.org/plc/ (accessed July 29, 2013).

Center on the Social and Emotional Foundations for Early Learning (CSEFEL). 2006. "Module 1: Promoting Children's Success: Building Relationships and Creating Supportive Environments." PowerPoint slides. http://csefel.vanderbilt.edu/resources/training_preschool.html (accessed July 29, 2013).

Clark, B. A. 2000. *First- and Second-Language Acquisition in Early Childhood.* http://ceep.crc.uiuc.edu/pubs/katzsym/clark-b.pdf (accessed July 29, 2013).

Coleman, R., and C. Goldenberg. 2012. "The Common Core Challenge for English Language Learners." *Principal Leadership,* February 2012. http://www.nassp.org/Content/158/pl_feb12_goldenberg.pdf (accessed July 29, 2013).

Colker, L. 2008. "Twelve Characteristics of Effective Early Childhood Teachers." *Young Children* 63:68–73.

Committee for Children. 2011. "Early Learning Review of Research: Second Step Program." http://www.cfchildren.org/Portals/0/SS_EL/EL_DOC/EL_Review_Research_SS.pdf (accessed July 30, 2013).

Conn-Powers, M., A. F. Cross, E. K. Traub, and L. Hutter-Pishgahi. 2006. "The Universal Design of Early Education: Moving Forward for All Children." *Beyond the Journal (Young Children on the Web),* September 2006. Washington, DC: National Association for the Education of Young Children. http://www.naeyc.org/files/yc/file/200609/ConnPowersBTJ.pdf (accessed July 30, 2013).

Copple, C. 2012. *Growing Minds: Building Strong Cognitive Foundations in Early Childhood.* Washington, DC: National Association for the Education of Young Children.

Copple, C., and S. Bredekamp, eds. 2009. *Developmentally Appropriate Practice in Early Childhood Serving Children from Birth Through*

REFERENCES

Age 8. 3rd ed. Washington, DC: National Association for the Education of Young Children.

Crane, T. 2007. *The Heart of Coaching: Using Transformational Coaching to Create a High-Performance Coaching Culture*. 2nd ed. San Diego, CA: FTA Press.

Curtis, D., and M. Carter. 2000. *The Art of Awareness: How Observation Can Transform Your Teaching*. St. Paul, MN: Redleaf Press.

———. 2003. *Designs for Living and Learning: Transforming Early Childhood Environments*. St. Paul, MN: Redleaf Press.

de Cos, P. 2001. *History and Development of Kindergarten in California*. Report prepared for the Joint Legislative Committee to develop a master plan for education (kindergarten through university). http://www.library.ca.gov/crb/01/03/01-003.pdf (accessed July 30, 2013).

Derman-Sparks, L., and J. O. Edwards. 2010. *Anti-Bias Education for Young Children and Ourselves*. Washington, DC: National Association for the Education of Young Children.

Division for Early Childhood (DEC) and National Association for the Education of Young Children (NAEYC). 2009. *Early Childhood Inclusion: A Joint Position Statement of the Division for Early Childhood (DEC) and the National Association for the Education of Young Children (NAEYC)*. Chapel Hill, NC: University of North Carolina at Chapel Hill, Frank Porter Graham Child Development Institute. http://npdci.fpg.unc.edu/resources/articles/Early_Childhood_Inclusion (accessed July 30, 2013).

Division for Early Childhood (DEC), National Association for the Education of Young Children (NAEYC), and National Head Start Association (NHSA). 2013. *Frameworks for Response to Intervention in Early Childhood: Description and Implications*. http://www.naeyc.org/files/naeyc/RTI%20in%20Early%20Childhood.pdf (accessed July 30, 2013).

Dodge, D. T., C. Heroman, J. Charles, and J. Maiorca. 2004. "Beyond Outcomes: How Ongoing Assessment Supports Children's Learning and Leads to Meaningful Curriculum." In *Spotlight on Young Children and Assessment*, edited by D. Koralek, 9–16. Washington, DC: National Association for the Education of Young Children.

Dombro, A. L., J. Jablon, and C. Stetson. 2011. *Powerful Interactions: How to Connect with Children to Extend Their Learning*. Washington, DC: National Association for the Education of Young Children.

Durlak, J. A., R. P. Weissberg, A. B. Dymnicki, and K. B. Schellinger. 2011. "The Impact of Enhancing Students' Social and Emotional Learning: A Meta-Analysis of School-Based Universal Interventions." *Child Development* 82 (1): 405–32.

The Education Alliance. 2008. *Professional Development—Excerpts from The Knowledge Loom: Educators Sharing and Learning Together*. Providence, RI: Brown University. http://knowledgeloom.org/pdf/KLOOM_pd_entire.pdf (accessed July 29, 2013).

Epstein, A. S. 2007. *The Intentional Teacher: Choosing the Best Strategies for Young Children's Learning*. Washington, DC: National Association for the Education of Young Children.

Epstein, J. L. 2001. *School and Family Partnerships: Preparing Educators and Improving Schools*. Boulder, CO: Westview Press.

Epstein, J. L., and S. B. Sheldon. 2006. "Moving Forward: Ideas for Research on School, Family, and Community Partnerships." In *The SAGE Handbook for Research in Education: Engaging Ideas and Enriching Inquiry*, edited by C. F. Conrad and R. C. Serlin, 117–138. Thousand Oaks, CA: Sage Publications.

Espinosa, L. M. 2010. *Getting it RIGHT for Young Children from Diverse Backgrounds: Applying Research to Improve Practices*. Upper Saddle River, NJ: Pearson Education.

Funkhouser, J. E., and M. R. Gonzales. 1997. *Family Involvement in Children's Education: Successful Local Approaches, An Idea Book*. Washington, DC: U.S. Government Printing Office.

Galinsky, E. 2010. *Mind in the Making: The Seven Essential Life Skills Every Child Needs*. New York: HarperCollins Publishers.

Gamm, S., J. Elliott, J. Wright Halbert, R. Price-Baugh, R. Hall, D. Walston, G. Uro, and M. Casserly. 2012. *Common Core State Standards and Diverse Urban Students: Using Multi-Tiered Systems of Support*. Washington, DC: Council of the Great City Schools. http://www.cgcs.org/site/default.aspx?PageType=3&ModuleInstanceID=312&ViewID=7b97f7ed-8e5e-4120-848f-a8b4987d588f&RenderLoc=0&FlexDataID=605&PageID=257 (accessed July 29, 2013).

Gartrell, D. 2007. "Guidance Matters: 'You Really Worked Hard on Your Picture!' Guiding with Encouragement." *Young Children* 62:50–52.

Gnadinger, C. M. 2008. "Peer-Mediated Instruction: Assisted Performance in the Primary Classroom." *Teachers and Teaching: Theory and Practice* 14 (2): 129–42.

Governor's Committee on Education Excellence. 2007. *Students First: Renewing Hope for California's Future*. http://everychildprepared.org/docs/summary.pdf (accessed July 30, 2013).

Graue, M. E., and J. DiPerna. 2000. "Redshirting and Early Retention: Who Gets the 'Gift of Time' and What Are Its Outcomes?" *American Educational Research Journal* 37:509–34.

Gullo, D. F. 2006. *Assessment in Kindergarten*. In *K Today: Teaching and Learning in the Kindergarten Year*, edited by D. F. Gullo, 138–147. Washington, DC: National Association for the Education of Young Children.

Guralnick, M. J. 1999. "The Nature and Meaning of Social Integration for Young Children with Mild Developmental Delays in Inclusive Settings." *Journal of Early Intervention* 22 (1): 70–86.

Hakuta, K., and M. Santos. 2012. *Understanding Language—Commissioned Papers on Language and Literacy Issues in the Common Core State Standards and Next Generation Science Standards*. Prepared for the Understanding Language Conference held on January 13–14, 2012, at Stanford University, Stanford, CA.

Harms, T., R. M. Clifford, and D. Cryer. 2005. *Early Childhood Environment Rating Scale*. Rev. ed. New York: Teachers College Press.

Heidemann, S., and D. Hewitt. 2010. *Play: The Pathway from Theory to Practice*. St. Paul, MN: Redleaf Press.

Henderson, A. T., and K. L. Mapp. 2002. *A New Wave of Evidence: The Impact of School, Family, and Community Connections on Student Achievement* (SEDL Annual Synthesis). Austin, TX: National Center for Family and Community Connections with Schools.

Heroman, C., and C. Copple. 2006. "Teaching in the Kindergarten Year." In *K Today: Teaching and Learning in the Kindergarten Year*, edited by D. F. Gullo, 59–72. Washington, DC: National Association for the Education of Young Children.

Hirsch, E. S. 1996. *The Block Book*. 3rd ed. Washington, DC: National Association for the Education of Young Children.

Hohmann, M., and D. P. Weikart. 2002. *Educating Young Children: Active Learning Practices for Preschool and Child Care Programs*. Ypsilanti, MI: HighScope Press.

Hohmann, M., D. P. Weikart, and A. S. Epstein. 2008. *Educating Young Children*. 3rd ed. Ypsilanti, MI: HighScope Press.

Hyson, M. 2004. *The Emotional Development of Young Children: Building an Emotion-Centered Curriculum*. 2nd ed. New York: Teachers College Press.

Individuals with Disabilities Education Act (IDEA). 2004. Part B, 20 U.S.C. § 1400. http://idea.ed.gov/ (accessed July 29, 2013).

Iowa School Boards Foundation. 2007. "Family, School and Community Connections: Improving Student Learning." Informational Briefing. http://www.ia-sb.org/assets/6822accf01e64833a1a3f99b1fddd217.pdf (accessed July 30, 2013).

Isbell, C., and R. Isbell. 2005. *The Inclusive Learning Center Book for Preschool Children with Special Needs*. Beltsville, MD: Gryphon House Inc.

Jablon, J. R., A. L. Dombro, and M. L. Dichtelmiller. 2007. *The Power of Observation for Birth Through Eight*. 2nd ed. Washington, DC: Teaching Strategies, Inc.

Jacobs, G., and K. Crowley. 2010. *Reaching Standards and Beyond in Kindergarten: Nurturing Children's Sense of Wonder and Joy in Learning*. Thousand Oaks, CA: Corwin Press.

Jalongo, M. R. 2004. *Young Children and Picture Books*. 2nd ed. Washington, DC: National Association for the Education of Young Children.

Jeynes, W. H. 2005. *Parental Involvement and Student Achievement: A Meta-Analysis* (Family Involvement Research Digests). Cambridge, MA: Harvard University Research Project.

Jones, J. 2004. "Framing the Assessment Discussion." In *Spotlight on Young Children and Assessment*, edited by D. Koralek, 4–8. Washington, DC: National Association for the Education of Young Children.

Justice, L. M., and P. C. Pullen. 2003. "Promising Interventions for Promoting Emergent Literacy Skills: Three Evidence-Based Approaches." *Topics in Early Childhood Special Education* 23:99–113.

Kaczmarek, L. A. 2007. "A Team Approach: Supporting Families of Children with Disabilities in Inclusive Programs." In *Spotlight on Young Children and Families*, edited by D. Koralek, 28–37. Washington, DC: National Association for the Education of Young Children.

Katz, L. G. 1995. "The Benefits of Mixed-Age Grouping." *Early Childhood and Parenting Collaborative*. http://ecap.crc.illinois.edu/eecearchive/digests/1995/lkmag95.html (accessed July 30, 2013).

———. 2000. "Academic Redshirting and Young Children." Educational Resource Information Center (U.S. Department of Education). http://www.education.com/print/Ref_Academic_Young/ (accessed July 30, 2013).

Kemp, C., and M. Carter. 2005. "Identifying Skills for Promoting Successful Inclusion in Kindergarten." *Journal of Intellectual and Developmental Disability* 30 (1): 31–34.

Koralek, D., and G. Mindes, eds. 2006. *Spotlight on Young Children and Social Studies*. Washington, DC: National Association for the Education of Young Children.

Lester, N. C. 2005. "Assessment in Multiage Primary Classrooms." *Issues in Educational Research* 15:145–55.

Louv, R. 2005. *Last Child in the Woods: Saving Our Children from Nature-Deficit Disorder*. Chapel Hill, NC: Algonquin Books of Chapel Hill.

Maxwell, K. L., and R. M. Clifford. 2004. "Research in Review: School Readiness Assessment." In *Spotlight on Young Children and Assessment*, edited by D. Koralek, 29–37. Washington, DC: National Association for the Education of Young Children.

McDevitt, T. M., and J. E. Ormrod. 2004. *Child Development: Educating and Working with Children and Adolescents*. 2nd ed. Upper Saddle River, NJ: Pearson Education, Inc.

Miller, E., and J. Almon. 2009. *Crisis in the Kindergarten: Why Children Need to Play in School*. College Park, MD: Alliance for Childhood.

Moss, B. 2003. *Exploring the Literature of Fact: Children's Nonfiction Trade Books in the Elementary Classroom*. New York: The Guilford Press.

Mueller, C. M., and C. S. Dweck. 1998. "Praise for Intelligence Can Undermine Children's Motivation and Performance." *Journal of Personality and Social Psychology* 75:33–52.

Musgrove, M. 2012. Policy letter dated February 29, 2012, on least restrictive environment (LRE) requirements in the Individuals with Disabilities Education Act (IDEA). Washington, DC: U.S. Department of Education, Office of Special Education and Rehabilitative Services. http://www2.ed.gov/policy/speced/guid/idea/memosdcltrs/preschoollre22912.pdf (accessed July 30, 2013).

Nagel, N., and J. Wells. 2009. "Honoring Family and Culture: Learning from New Zealand." *Young Children* 64:40–44.

National Center for Learning Disabilities (NCLD). 2009. *Roadmap to Pre-K RTI: Applying Response to Intervention in Preschool Settings*. New York: National Center for Learning Disabilities. http://www.rtinetwork.org/images/roadmaptoprekrti.pdf (accessed July 30, 2013).

———. 2013. "Multi-Tier System of Supports, aka Response to Intervention (RTI)." Issue Brief. http://www.ncld.org/images/content/files/hill-briefs/mtss-brief-template.pdf (accessed July 31, 2013).

National Coalition for Parent Involvement in Education (NCPIE). 2006. "A New Wave of Evidence: The Impact of School, Family and Community Connections on Student Achievement." http://www.ncpie.org/pubs/NewWaveofEvidenceJan2003.pdf (accessed July 30, 2013).

National Institute for Early Education Research. 2004. "Preschool Assessment: A Guide to Developing a Balanced Approach." *Preschool Policy Matters* 7. http://nieer.org/resources/policybriefs/7.pdf (accessed July 29, 2013).

National Institute of Child Health and Human Development (NICHD) Early Child Care Research Network. 2003. "Do Children's Attention Processes Mediate the Link Between Family Predictors and School Readiness?" *Developmental Psychology* 39:581–93.

National Professional Development Center on Inclusion (NPDCI). 2012. *Response to Intervention (RTI) in Early Childhood: Building Consensus on the Defining Features*. Chapel Hill, NC: University of North Carolina at Chapel Hill, Frank Porter Graham Child Development Institute. http://www.fpg.unc.edu/sites/default/files/resources/reports-and-policy-briefs/NPDCI-RTI-Concept-Paper_2012.pdf (accessed July 30, 2013).

National Research Council. 2001. *Eager to Learn: Educating Our Preschoolers*. Washington, DC: The National Academies Press.

National Research Council and Institute of Medicine. 2000. *From Neurons to Neighborhoods: The Science of Early Childhood Development*. Washington, DC: The National Academies Press.

Nature Explore. 2011. *Growing with Nature: Supporting Whole-Child Learning in Outdoor Classrooms*. Lincoln, NE: Dimensions Educational Research Foundation.

Neisworth, J. T., and S. J. Bagnato. 2005. "DEC Recommended Practices: Assessment." In *DEC Recommended Practices: A Comprehensive Guide for Practical Application in Early Intervention/Early Childhood Special Education*, 45–69. Longmont, CO: Sopris West Educational Services.

Nemeth, K. N. 2012. *Basics of Supporting Dual Language Learners: An Introduction for Educators of Children Birth Through Age 8*. Washington, DC: National Association for the Education of Young Children.

Nielsen, L. 2009. *Adaptations in Action: Adaptation Bin for Children* (ABC). San Jose, CA: Santa Clara County Office of Education. http://www.sccoe. org/depts/students/inclusion-collaborative/ Documents/Adaptations%20in%20Action%20 Book.pdf (accessed July 30, 2013).

Odom, S. L. 2000. "Preschool Inclusion: What We Know and Where We Want to Go from Here." *Topics in Early Childhood Special Education* 20 (1): 20–27.

Odom, S. L., V. Buysse, and E. Soukakou. 2011. "Inclusion for Young Children with Disabilities: A Quarter Century of Research Perspectives." *Journal of Early Intervention* 33 (4): 344–56.

Pianta, R. C. 2011. *Teaching Children Well: New Evidence-Based Approaches to Teacher Professional Development and Training*. Washington, DC: Center for American Progress. http://www.americanprogress.org/ issues/2011/11/pdf/piana_report.pdf (accessed July 30, 2013).

Pianta, R. C., and M. E. Kraft-Sayre. 2003. *Successful Kindergarten Transitions: Your Guide to Connecting Children, Families, and Schools*. Baltimore, MD: Brookes Publishing.

Pianta, R. C., and M. Stuhlman. 2004. "Teacher–Child Relationships and Children's Success in the First Years of School." *School Psychology Review* 33 (3): 444–58.

Ranweiler, L. W. 2004. *Preschool Readers and Writers: Early Literacy Strategies for Teachers*. Ypsilanti, MI: HighScope Press.

Raver, C. C. 2002. "Emotions Matter: Making a Case for the Role of Young Children's Emotional Development for Early School Readiness." *Social Policy Report of the Society for Research in Child Development* 16 (3): 1–20.

Raver, C. C., and J. Knitzer. 2002. *Ready to Enter: What Research Tells Policymakers About Strategies to Promote Social and Emotional School Readiness Among Three-and Four-Year-Olds*. New York: National Center for Children in Poverty.

Riley, D., R. R. San Juan, J. Klinkner, and A. Ramminger. 2008. *Social and Emotional Development: Connecting Science and Practice in Early Childhood Settings*. St. Paul, MN: Redleaf Press.

Ritchie, S., K. L. Maxwell, and S. Bredekamp. 2009. "Rethinking Early Schooling: Using Developmental Science to Transform Children's Early School Experiences." In *Handbook of Child Development and Early Education: Research to Practice*, edited by O. A. Barbarin and B. H. Wasik, 14–37. New York: The Guilford Press.

Rivkin, M. S. 1995. *The Great Outdoors: Restoring Children's Right to Play Outside*. Washington, DC: National Association for the Education of Young Children.

Rosenow, N. 2008. "Learning to Love the Earth . . . and Each Other." *Young Children* 63:10–13.

Ross, E. D. 1976. *The Kindergarten Crusade: The Establishment of Preschool Education in the United States*. Athens, OH: Ohio University Press.

Sadao, K. C., and N. B. Robinson. 2010. *Assistive Technology with Young Children: Creating Inclusive Learning Environments*. Baltimore MD: Brookes Publishing.

Sanders, S. 2002. *Active for Life: Developmentally Appropriate Movement Programs for Young Children*. Champaign, IL: Human Kinetics.

Seefeldt, C., and A. Galper. 2006. *Active Experiences for Active Children: Social Studies*. 2nd ed. Upper Saddle River, NJ: Pearson Education.

Seplocha, H. 2007. "Partnerships for Learning: Conferencing with Families." In *Spotlight on Young Children and Families*, edited by D. Koralek, 12–15. Washington, DC: National Association for the Education of Young Children.

Shillady, A. 2004. "Choosing an Appropriate Assessment System." In *Spotlight on Young Children and Families*, edited by D. Koralek, 54–57. Washington, DC: National Association for the Education of Young Children.

Siraj-Blatchford, I., K. Sylva, S. Muttock, R. Gilden, and D. Bell. 2002. *Researching Effective Pedagogy in the Early Years*. Research Report No. 356. Norwich, United Kingdom: Queen's Printer. http://dera.ioe.ac.uk/4650/1/RR356.pdf (accessed July 30, 2013).

Smith, B. J. 2010. *Recommended Practices: Linking Social Development and Behavior to School Readiness*. Nashville, TN: Center on the Social and Emotional Foundations for Early Learning.

Smith, M. W. 2001. "Children's Experiences in Preschool." In *Beginning Literacy with Language: Young Children Learning at Home and School*, edited by D. K. Dickinson and P. O. Tabors, 149–74. Baltimore, MD: Paul H. Brookes Publishing Co.

Southwest Educational Development Laboratory (SEDL). 1997. "Professional Learning Communities: What Are They and Why Are They Important?" *Issues . . . about Change* 6 (1). http://www.sedl.org/change/issues/issues61.html (accessed July 30, 2013).

Sugarman, N. A. 2011. "Putting Yourself in Action: Individual Professional Development Plans." *Young Children* 66:27–33.

Tabors, P. O., and C. S. Snow. 2001. "Young Bilingual Children and Early Literacy Development." In *Handbook of Early Literacy Research: Volume 1*, edited by S. B. Neuman and D. K. Dickinson, 159–78. New York: The Guilford Press.

Thompson, J. E., and R. A. Thompson. 2007. "Natural Connections: Children, Nature, and Social–Emotional Development." *Child Care Information Exchange* 11/12 (2007): 46–50.

Thompson, J. E., and K. K. Twibell. 2009. "Teaching Hearts and Minds in Early Childhood Classrooms: Curriculum for Social and Emotional Development." In *Children of 2020: Creating a Better Tomorrow*, edited by V. Washington and J. Andrews, 199–222. Washington, DC: Council for Professional Recognition.

Thompson, R. A., and M. Goodman. 2009. "Development of Self, Relationships, and Socioemotional Competence: Foundations for Early School Success." In *Handbook of Child Development and Early Education: Research to Practice*, edited by O. A. Barbarin and B. H. Wasik, 147–71. New York: The Guilford Press.

Tomalison, H. B. 2009. "Developmentally Appropriate Practice in the Kindergarten Year—Ages-5-6: An Overview." In *Developmentally Appropriate Practice in Early Childhood Programs: Serving Children from Birth Through Age 8*, edited by C. Copple and S. Bredekamp, 186–253. Washington, DC: National Association for the Education of Young Children.

Twibell, K., and D. Harkins. forthcoming. "Beyond Nature Hikes and Butterflies: Expanding Children's Capacity for Scientific Inquiry." *Exchange Magazine* (scheduled for publication in September/October 2013).

U.S. Department of Education. 2006. Improving Teacher Quality State Grants—Elementary and Secondary Education Act (ESEA) of 1965, Title II, Part A, Non-regulatory guidance. http://www2.ed.gov/programs/teacherqual/legislation.html (accessed July 30, 2013).

Ventura County Office of Education and California Department of Education. 2011. *Response to Instruction and Intervention (RtI²): An Implementation and Technical Assistance Guide for Districts and Schools*. Sacramento: California Department of Education. http://www.cde.ca.gov/ci/cr/ri/ (accessed July 30, 2013).

Wasik, B. 2008. "When Fewer Is More: Small Groups in Early Childhood Classrooms." *Early Education Journal* 35:515–21.

Watson, A., and R. McCathren. 2009. "Including Children with Special Needs: Are You and Your Early Childhood Program Ready?" *Beyond the Journal (Young Children on the Web)*, March 2009. Washington, DC: National Association for the Education of Young Children. http://journal.naeyc.org/btj/200903/pdf/BTJWatson.pdf (accessed July 30, 2013).

Weissbourd, B., R. Weissbourd, and K. O'Carroll. 2010. "Family Engagement." In *Children of 2020: Creating a Better Tomorrow*, edited by V. Washington and J. Andrews, 114–18. Washington, DC: Council for Professional Recognition.

Wells, G. 2009. "The Social Context of Language and Literacy Development." In *Handbook of Child Development and Early Education: Research to Practice*, edited by O. A. Barbarin and B. H. Wasik, 271–302. New York: The Guilford Press.

Yoon, K. S., T. Duncan, S. Wen-Yu Lee, B. Scarloss, and K. Shapley. 2007. *Reviewing the Evidence on How Teacher Professional Development Affects Student Achievement*. Issues & Answers Report, REL 2007, No. 033. Washington, DC: U.S. Department of Education, Institute of Education Sciences, National Center for Education Evaluation and Regional Assistance, Regional Educational Laboratory. http://ies.ed.gov/ncee/edlabs/regions/southwest/pdf/rel_2007033.pdf (accessed July 30, 2013).

York, S. 2003. *Roots and Wings: Affirming Culture in Early Childhood Programs*. Rev. ed. St. Paul, MN: Red Leaf Press.

Zins, J., M. Bloodworth, R. Weissberg, and H. Walberg. 2004. "The Scientific Base Linking Social and Emotional Learning to School Success." In *Building Academic Success on Social Emotional Learning: What Does the Research Say?*, edited by J. Zins, R. Weissberg, M. Wang, and H. J. Walberg, 1–22. New York: Teachers Press, Columbia University.